P9-CKP-709

꙰ Women in Korean Zen

Women in Religion

Amanda Porterfield and Mary Farrell Bednarowski, Series Editors

Martine Batchelor as a nun, with Son'gyong Sunim, and Songgwangsa
monastery. Photographs by Stephen Batchelor.

Women in Korean Zen

LIVES AND PRACTICES

Martine Batchelor and Son'gyong Sunim

SYRACUSE UNIVERSITY PRESS

Copyright © 2006 by Syracuse University Press
Syracuse, New York, 13244–5160
All Rights Reserved

First Edition 2006
06 07 08 09 10 11   6 5 4 3 2 1

Portions of Part 2 were previously published in *Women on the Buddhist Path*
(2002). Permission to reprint has been granted by HarperCollins Publishers
Ltd. and is gratefully acknowledged.

The paper used in this publication meets the minimum requirements of
American National Standard for Information Sciences—Permanence of
Paper for Printed Library Materials, ANSI Z39.48–1984.∞™

Library of Congress Cataloging-in-Publication Data

Batchelor, Martine.
Women in Korean Zen : lives and practices / Martine Batchelor and
Son'gyong Sunim.—1st ed.
p. cm.—(Women in religion)
Includes bibliographical references.
ISBN 0-8156-0842-X (alk. paper)
1. Batchelor, Martine. 2. Spiritual biography—France. 3. Spiritual
biography—Korea (South) 4. Monastic and religious life (Zen
Buddhism)—Korea (South) 5. Monastic and religious life of women—
Korea (South) 6. Buddhist nuns—Korea (South) I. Sön'gyöng, Sunim,
1903–1994. II. Title. III. Series: Women in religion (Syracuse University)
BQ942.A688A3   2005
294.3'927092—dc22   2005026591

Manufactured in the United States of America

To the memory of Son'gyong Sunim
and Hyonum Sunim

Martine Batchelor was a Zen Buddhist nun in South Korea for ten years. She left the monastic life in 1985 and returned to live in Europe. Her books include *Principles of Zen, Women on the Buddhist Path, Meditation for Life* (an illustrated book on meditation), and *The Path of Compassion* (a translation of the Bodhisattva Precepts). With her husband, Stephen Batchelor, she co-leads meditation retreats worldwide. They currently live in France.

Son'gyong Sunim was born in 1903 to a peasant family in Korea. At age eighteen she joined Yongunam Nunnery. She remained a Buddhist Zen nun all her life, eventually becoming the leader of the Zen hall at Naewonsa. She died in 1994.

Contents

Living as a Zen Nun | *Martine Batchelor*

Seeking the Way | *Son'gyong Sunim*

～ Illustrations

Acknowledgments

I WOULD LIKE TO THANK deeply all the foreign monks and nuns of Songgwangsa, specially Haehaeng, Haemyong, Hamwol, Jagwang, Jigwang, and Suil. I am grateful to the monks and the *bosalnim*s of Songgwangsa and Poplyonsa, especially Chonghak Sunim, Hyonbong Sunim, Hyonho Sunim, Hyonji Sunim, Hyonmuk Sunim, Hyonmun Sunim, Popjong Sunim, Posong Sunim, Yongjin Sunim, Yongjo Sunim, and Yongson Sunim. I am indebted to the nuns of Huiryongsa, Hunglyunsa, Hungyongsa, Myongpopsa, Naewonsa, P'alchongsa, Podoksa, Taewonsa, Unmunsa, especially Haehae Sunim, Haeju Sunim, Myongsong Sunim, Popin Sunim, and Songou Sunim, and also Pomyong Sunim, Myoljin Sunim, Jiwon Sunim, Jiyong Sunim, and Tokang Sunim. I benefited greatly from the teachings of the late Master Doksan, the late Master Haeam, the late Master Kyongbong, Venerable Shig hiu Wan, and Master Songdam. I appreciated the heartfelt and kind support of Korean laypeople, especially the Kim family, Myolyonhwa Bosalnim, and Mandokchang Bosalnim. I thank Professor Cho, Professor Park, and Professor Hsieh for sharing their conference papers with me. The Ash Family, Stephen Batchelor, Bolishim Bosalnim, Diana St. Ruth, Hyunghi May, Professor Hwang, and Professor Jang helped me greatly. I am grateful to Brian McCord and the team at Syracuse University Press for their enthusiasm for this book.

✼ Introduction

FROM 1975 TO 1985, I spent ten years as a Buddhist Zen nun in Korea. I was one of the few Western nuns in the country at that time. My situation was somewhat unusual and my experiences not exactly identical to those of a Korean nun. However, I had many opportunities to live closely with them and become part of their communities. In the first part of this book, I try to present what the life of a Zen nun is like through my own experiences. This description should provide the necessary context for the second part of the book, the autobiography of a respected Korean Zen nun, Son'gyong Sunim (1903–1994).

A FRENCH LIFE

I was raised in a French family living in the countryside. My father was an engineer who built dams. As soon as one dam was finished he went to work on another, so we moved all over France. From an early age I wanted to travel and explore the world. My parents were committed humanists who were, and are still, suspicious of religion. In my teens I was concerned about the state of the world and interested in politics. I had dreams of becoming a journalist.

At the age of eighteen, however, a look at the *Dhammapada,* a collection of the Buddha's recommendations for living a good life, at a friend's house was a turning point for me. When I read that it might be better to change oneself before thinking of changing the world, it made sense. So I turned away from politics and became interested in meditation. Then at age twenty-two in 1975, after gathering five hundred dollars doing odd jobs, I was finally able to travel to Asia, and I ended up in Korea. To live for ten years in Korea was to penetrate a different culture and society and to discover the meaning of a meditative practice and the religious life. It was a journey of discovery of myself, of a country, of a people.

SON'GYONG SUNIM

The nunnery in Korea with which I had the strongest connection was Naewonsa, near Pusan, where Son'gyong Sunim was the leader of the meditation hall. I was deeply moved by and drawn to her humility and kindness, strength and wisdom, and would visit her regularly. She was tiny and stooped but remarkably energetic for her eighty years. My first inclination upon meeting her was always to give her a big hug, but the customs of Korean Buddhist nunneries prevented such behavior. She was very respected and much loved by the community because, as I learned while living there, she had developed the qualities of wisdom and compassion that come from a long cultivation of meditation. When she was not leading the meditation in the Zen hall, following a daily schedule of ten hours of sitting and walking meditation, she would be busy gathering acorns or performing other chores for the community.

The more I got to know her, the more I appreciated her way of being, and that made me want to know more about her sixty years of life as a nun. I also thought her story would be inspiring for other people. So over a two-year period, from 1980 to 1982, she dictated her life story to me, and I recorded it. It was a delight to listen to her relate her experiences, laughing here and there at this or that adventure. I hope my translation conveys the sense of joy, openness, and lightness that is so much a part of her.

Her life spans the twentieth century. It is a bridge between the life of old Korea and new Korea, before the Korean War and after the Korean War. As I heard her stories and experiences I was taken to a different time, when life was extremely hard and poor and where one had visions and mystical dreams. When Son'gyong Sunim was born, 1903, the Korean Confucian Dynasty was in its last throes before being taking over by the

Japanese in 1910. Being born into a poor peasant family meant that there really was no chance for her to develop and elevate herself in this very stratified Confucian society. Her only faint glimmer of hope for change was in becoming a Zen Buddhist nun. Her life illustrates the development that occurred for Korean nuns in the last century, from meager resources to well-supported conditions.

The life of Son'gyong Sunim is an inspiration and an example of developing one's potential and abilities. There is no doubt that her physical and psychological makeup shows her to be humble and self-deprecating, but nevertheless, repeatedly she aspires and achieves what seems to be beyond her or beyond what she could hope for or think of. She expresses some regrets about her failure to do or complete certain actions, which might have enabled her to achieve full awakening. And these regrets fit a pattern of self-criticism, but every time she changes situation, she is trying to move forward and to explore different possibilities.

It seems to me her being is her awakening, and her poems express this clearly. They are evocative, pithy, and direct and show fully her power as a realized woman.

A SHORT HISTORICAL SURVEY

Buddhism entered Korea in the fourth century. Until the twelfth century, Buddhism was supported by the state and had a strong following among the people. However, the Koryo Dynasty fell in 1392, and Buddhism declined with the advent of the Choson period (1392–1910), which adopted Neo-Confucianism as the prevailing ideology for the country. The Choson rulers tried to restrict the spread of Buddhism: temples could not be built near towns but had to be constructed in the mountains; monks and nuns could not enter the capital and had to wear large hats to cover their faces when they went out. Yet in spite of such restrictions, the order of nuns survived.

In 1910 Korea was annexed as a colony of Japan. Although the Japanese favored Buddhism, they tried to impose their own forms of the religion, including the tradition of married clergy who were put in charge of the main temples. This change made it difficult for the celibate monks and nuns. Since the defeat of the Japanese in 1945, there has been a great revival of Korean Buddhism, halted only by the Korean War, during which time many monks and nuns had to go undercover and wear lay clothing to avoid arrest by the communists. Since the armistice with North Korea in 1953, nuns have been a strong force in the restoration of the religion, even converting abandoned monasteries into nunneries with Sutra halls for the study of Buddhist doctrine and Zen halls for the practice of meditation.

KOREAN ZEN NUNS

Few are aware of the great number of fully ordained Buddhist nuns *(pikkuni/bhiksuni)* living in Korea. People often are surprised that Buddhist nuns exist at all, not to mention fully ordained Zen nuns with virtually the same status in their society as monks, living in their own independent and thriving nunneries. In this book I want to show how a strong *bhiksuni* tradition has survived in Korea over many centuries and has proved to be both durable and adaptable to changing times.

Two thousand five hundred years ago in India, the Buddha was reluctant to ordain women. His close personal attendant, Ananda, pointed out that if the Buddha proclaimed the equality of men and women in terms of spiritual accomplishments, why could not women become Buddhist mendicants as well? So the Buddha relented and started to ordain women. They shaved their heads, wore saffron and depended on alms. As Buddhism spread in the Indian subcontinent it reached Sri Lanka, and a strong order of Buddhist nuns developed in that country. This order died out in the tenth century CE and was never reconstituted. However in the fifth century CE, Sri Lankan nuns had gone to China by sea and transmitted the full ordination to Chinese nuns, which has been preserved to this day and has also spread to Korea

The mentions of Korean nuns in historical records are relatively rare but they do appear. For example it is recorded that in 577, the Korean (Paekje) King Widok sent various texts, artisans, and *bhiksunis* to Japan. In 655, Bhiksuni Popmyong is said to have gone to Japan and is reputed to have cured a sick person by chanting the *Vimalakirtinirdesa Sutra*. There are records of queens and aristocratic ladies becoming *bhiksunis* like Bhiksuni Myopop, who was the wife of (Shilla) King Pophung (r. 514–546). Bhiksuni Sasin (1694–1765) was recorded as being "renowned for donations and building projects." Korean culture being very patriarchal, one cannot be surprised at the lack of written information.

In 2004 there are about ten thousand nuns (*bhiksunis* and *sramanerikas*) in Korea. Every year about a hundred novices (*sramanerikas*) and a hundred *bhiksunis* are ordained. Novices take 10 precepts and *bhiksunis* 348. The Koreans follow the Dharmagupta tradition of *Vinaya* (Rule of discipline), which was brought to the country from China and originally came from India. In total there are about eight hundred nunneries and hermitages for nuns in Korea, which include thirty-five Zen halls. Although living independent lives, the nuns until recently did not have access to the higher echelons of the Buddhist University or of the Chogye Order Headquarter, but this has changed. At the time of writing (2004), one *bhiksuni* has been nominated director (of culture) in the Chogye Order administration, two other nuns occupy position in this administration, and there are four *bhiksuni* professors at the Buddhist University of Dongguk in Seoul.

The lives of the nuns are also changing with the times. When I arrived in Korea in 1975, the country was still very poor, which was reflected in the poverty of the temples themselves, their supporters not being able to give them much financial help. Over the ten years I lived there, I could see the standards of living in Korea rise for the people and the temples, as Korean people are very generous to their religion. By the time I returned for a visit in 1992, the standards had risen again, and I found public phones in all major temples. Twelve years later, Korea has further modernized, as have the nunneries. Most nunneries have hot showers and gas fires in their kitchens, as does Songgwangsa, where nowadays many monks own and drive cars. In 2004, although the temples have considerably modernized, the same ancient and proven schedules of practice are followed in the Zen halls and similar programs of studies in the seminaries.

In Korea the nuns are as respected as the monks, and so are well supported financially by their followers. Nowadays nuns have bank accounts and some have substantial wealth. The tenth precept of novices (not accumulating gold and silver) is interpreted more liberally in Korea, a Mahayana Buddhist country, than in the Theravada countries of Sri Lanka and Southeast Asia. Generally nuns will use their wealth to create education facilities for laypeople or nuns and support welfare projects. Nowadays *bhiksuni*s manage thirty welfare facilities, including children's welfare, elder care, women's welfare, and medical welfare. They also try to renovate their nunneries. Moreover, senior nuns are now able to send their disciples to university in Korea or abroad. Korean nuns can also fulfill a long-cherished dream to go on pilgrimage to the original Buddhist sites in India with their lay followers. Until the 1980s, most Koreans could not leave the country because of a lack of resources and political restrictions. Now that these two obstacles have been removed, one of the greatest joys of Korean Buddhist women is to travel in Buddhist countries guided by their leading nun.

MOTIVATION

When a young Korean women wants to become a nun, her motivation might come from different sources. If she comes from a Buddhist family, she has been familiar with Buddhism and the temple life from an early age. For example, Pomyong Sunim entered the nunnery when she was five years old. She was very ill; her family believed that she was going to die and that only by being sent to live in a Buddhist temple would she survive. When I met her in 1992, she had been a nun for thirty-two years. She had remained after she was cured because she liked the nunnery life so much. She had no regrets and planned to stay a nun all her life.

A young woman might be compelled to become a nun by some burning question. A nun friend, Myoljin Sunim, when she was young, used to wonder: "Why do we live?" and wanted to understand the origin of life. She decided to investigate biology and microorganisms, so she studied cytology. Although she looked deeply, she could not find anything. Then she met a Zen Buddhist who told her that through practicing Zen meditation she would understand and discover the answer to her question. By awakening, she would know herself and the essence of life.

During one holiday she went to a temple and decided to meditate very hard, hoping to complete her search by the end of that summer. One day suddenly everything became obvious, and she had an intellectual answer to all her questions. Explanations kept on rolling inside her mind, and it was so marvelous and fascinating that she kept sitting all day and night. She felt she was making a mistake, however, as the answers were only intellectual and her ideas kept revolving in a vacuum. And she developed painful headaches. She went to the master, who told her to relax and encouraged her to go beyond all these intellectual answers.

Sometimes women become nuns because of some difficulties, as a last resort, as in the case of Son'gyong Sunim, who was in great poverty and distress and thinking of suicide, and decided instead to try to be a nun for a while. In other cases, female students go to Buddhist classes and are touched by the nuns. To them the nuns look so clean and pure, and what they teach makes so much sense. Sometimes a student is impressed by a nun and wants to become like her. In the end, every nun has her own specific reasons for becoming a nun. These women who choose to become nuns often have been different in their childhood, questioning eating meat, for example. Although their parents do not like them to live celibate lives, they are not surprised by their choice of vocation. The nuns rarely regret the life outside and say that they do not long for it. Once a friend, Jiwon Sunim, told me that she became so upset in her first year at the nunnery that she took the bus and left for town. Once she got there, however, she looked around and realized it was not what she wanted, so she came back the same day.

Owing to a long tradition of Confucianism, men and women have clearly differentiated roles in Korean society. First a woman is expected to serve her father, then her husband, then her son. In the cities especially, women tend to be quite feminine and delicate. However, these expectations and tendencies are absent in the nunneries. With the nuns, one feels one is meeting human beings who have been able to develop their full potential, integrating both their female and male sides. For many Korean women, to become a nun is not a restriction but a liberation.

La Sauve 2005   Martine Batchelor

Living as a Zen Nun

Martine Batchelor

Martine Batchelor as a nun, with Master Kusan.
Photograph by Stephen Batchelor.

～ Arrival in Korea

"CLAP!" The old Zen monk slapped my palm. "Where did the sound go?" he asked. Dumbfounded, I could not answer and just sat there in a bemused state. I was wearing gray clothes and my head was shaved and shining. I was sitting in a small Korean hermitage in front of one of the most respected Korean Zen masters, Master Kyongbong.

I was perplexed and would remain perplexed for the following ten years. For that is the aim of Korean Zen practice: to make you more and more perplexed. It challenges you to question and marvel at the mystery of being alive. It all started with a question as well: "How could I change the world? How could I make it a better place to live for everyone?" I found the answer in the words of the Buddha, who said, "Before transforming others, you must transform yourself." This raised another question: "How could I transform myself?" Meditation seemed to be the answer. So I started on a long journey that led me from being an anarchist and somewhat hippie in 1970s France to Korea, and the life of a Zen nun, where every day, at all times, I was encouraged to ask: "Why did Chaochou say 'No'?"

I came to Korea by accident. I wanted to go from Bangkok in Thailand to Osaka and Tokyo in Japan but instead was issued a ticket for Seoul in Korea and Tokyo. Then, again by accident, I met a Korean monk in a Thai temple who extolled the virtues of meditation practice in Korean Zen monasteries and nunneries. So I decided to visit the country for a month on my way to Japan. It took ten years for me finally to reached Japan—and I only stayed there for two months.

That short experience in Japanese Zen monasteries made me understand what was meant by the Zen saying that people's different affinities match different types of Buddhist training. I do not think I could have remained long in Japan. It felt too strict and severe for me. During the summer retreats the windows are closed in the meditation hall, so you are uncomfortably hot. In winter the windows are open, so you are uncomfortably cold. The only way to stand this discomfort is through total concentration in meditation. Then you cease to be bothered by the extremes of temperature. But in Korea the stone floors of the meditation hall are heated in winter and the doors left wide open in summer. You feel physically at ease and yet, at least in my case, all the more able to concentrate on your meditation.

If you move ever so slightly or nod in a Japanese meditation hall, you are hit on the shoulder with a flat wooden stick and are grateful for it. In Korea, the stick was abandoned in favor of independence. You are in the meditation hall because you want to meditate, to awaken; it is up to you to be as aware as possible and put in as much effort as you can. Koreans being the way they are, they would probably argue that they were neither moving nor about to fall asleep and would resent being struck with a stick. Both methods doubtless bring results and can be useful for different people. Fortunately for me, I believe, I ended up in Korea.

The monk I met in Thailand had given me the address of a nunnery called Sognamsa, situated deep in the southernmost part of South Korea. The nunnery stood in a quiet valley near a river that flowed though lush green mountains. Hesitantly, I passed through two large and imposing wooden doors. Inside was a courtyard surrounded by small buildings with beautiful tiled roofs. The corners of the roofs turned up slightly, like birds about to launch into flight. In the middle of the courtyard stood a graceful four-tiered *stupa* (reliquary); at one side of that, on an elevated bank, was an elegant building that rose proudly above the others. Its walls and eaves were brightly painted with various motifs, and its wooden latticework and paper doors were decorated in delicate flower designs. This building was the main Buddha hall.

The only nun who spoke any English took me for a walk. I tried to ask her some questions about Buddhism and meditation, but her English was too limited for her to answer properly. As we walked along the river, which shimmered in the soft evening light, she nevertheless managed to convey that a good meditator was able to hold a conversation and to meditate at the same time. I was very impressed by that remark.

That evening I attended a service in the main Buddha hall. In the middle of the hall was a large platform, on top of which sat a golden Buddha. Behind the Buddha was a colorful painting representing buddhas and bodhisattvas and in front of it stood an incense burner, a bowl of water, and two candles. I was to learn that the incense and the candles were symbols of selflessness because they consume themselves while giving out fragrance and light, and the water was a symbol of purity and nonattachment because it reflects everything else.

As it was the first such service I had ever attended, I just did as the others did. To begin with everything went fine; we bowed while chanting, then chanted while standing still. Then when it seemed to be over, we bowed without chanting and bowed and bowed and kept on bowing. It seemed as if it would never end, and my knees started to give way. Finally the bowing stopped, and I hobbled back to my room. The night was black and quiet, save for the hooting of an owl. Later I learned that the nuns bowed 108 times every evening as an act of purification and as a way of bestowing merits on others.

This service was my first encounter with bowing, and I must say it did not endear me to it. Thereafter I avoided it as much as possible. Only once did I understand what it was about. On one occasion I could not avoid having to bow 108 times with a few other people. During the first 30, I was full of resentment: "This is ridiculous. What I am doing this for? Why 108 anyway?" But when I reached number 35, suddenly all the resentment and chatter dropped away, and I just bowed in a flowing motion with great awareness and clarity. But I never tried it again. Some blocks are very persistent.

At dawn a nun walked around the courtyard chanting, marking the tempo by beating a small, hollowed piece of wood shaped like a bell. It was struck with a wooden stick and made a sort of high-pitched yet mellow sound. Then came the deep ring of a great metal bell. This bell was struck with a huge log and called everyone to the morning service. It was beautiful to be awoken by such sounds in the early dawn; it resonated with something deep within myself.

Breakfast consisted of rice, thin soup, hot pickles, and wild greens. Because I could not speak Korean and the nuns could not speak English, they decided after breakfast to send me to the only place in Korea at that time (1975) where Western monks were practicing Zen, the monastery of Songgwangsa, on the opposite corner of the peninsula.

The bus dropped me near the monastery, a group of buildings nestling at the foot of forested hills. The day of my arrival turned out to be the monastery's biggest annual Buddhist festival—the celebration of the birth of Master Puril Pojo (1158–1210), the great monk who founded the monastery in 1200. For three days, a thousand lay people and several hundred monks and nuns stayed at the monastery. They all came to take the bodhisattva precepts for the first time or to renew them (these vows are renewed every year) and to listen to lectures on Buddhism. The monks provided food three times a day, which always seemed to be the same rice, pickles, and greens that I had had for my first breakfast in the nunnery. Every room in the place was filled to capacity with sleeping people. The hard floors were heated by a system of flues and stonework, so it was not unpleasant to sleep on them.

I was shown to the guest rooms near the kitchen. The place was in great turmoil—people everywhere cleaning, cooking, transporting tables, and laying them with bowls, thin metal chopsticks, and spoons. Wanting to be of help, I joined a group of people who were tearing the top leaves off some vegetables that looked like a cross between celery and cress. I asked a monk why we were doing this, as the green tops must be full of vitamins. He replied that in Korea one did not eat them.

Later, after I had been in the monastery for some time, I began to see how conditioned I was and how deeply ingrained my cultural habits were. I often caught myself thinking that the French way was the right way, but

I soon realized that Koreans must be thinking the same about their way of doing things. Over the coming years, I was to learn how to wring clothes the proper way (the opposite of what I was used to), to sit without pointing my feet toward a Buddhist statue or another person, and always to present objects with two hands. To eat correctly, I had to finish every last grain and wash my bowl clean with rice-water and drink it. I had to learn to walk on wooden verandas softly without making noise (an arduous task for heavy-footed Westerners). It was essential to wash my upper bodily parts and clothes in a basin marked "up" and my lower bodily parts and clothes in a basin marked "down." I needed also to wash my shoes and socks every night. But I had not learned all these things yet, so I just sat cutting the tops off these strange looking vegetables and thinking of the wasted vitamins.

⤳ Meeting a Zen Master

THE NEXT MORNING one of the Western monks took a young American who had recently arrived and me to see Master Kusan, the Zen master of Songgwangsa. I had never met a Zen master before and went with great trepidation. We entered his room, which was an antechamber and a space separated by sliding inner doors. The doors were open, and there was no furniture except for a few cushions and a low desk. The floor was covered with varnished, yellow-ochre paper, which shone in the soft light penetrating the paper outer doors. We paid our respects by bowing three times in his direction, as previously instructed, and then sat and waited. He was sitting cross-legged on the floor, wearing the same sort of garb as everyone else—a simple gray jacket and baggy gray trousers. His face and shaven head shone, and he looked ageless to me. I was rather moved by his presence and assumed he was a tall man (I was surprised to discover later that he was actually smaller than I). He smiled warmly. There was a sparkle in his eyes as he began to ask us questions.

First he asked where we had come from and what was our nationality. Then with a penetrating gaze, he looked at me and said, "What is the most important thing in the world?"

I replied, "Two people smiling at each other."

He smiled. "Yes, that's good, but there is something even more important than that. You know your body, but do you know your true mind?"

I could not answer.

He then proceeded to encourage me to meditate by asking myself at all times, "What is this?"

Then he turned to the young American and said, "What is the most frightening thing in the world?"

"To walk alone in the dark at night."

The master laughed heartily. "No, there is something much more frightening than that: not to know your own mind." He then gave him the same question to investigate: "What is this?"

These questions are called *hwadu* in Korean. Master Kusan belonged to the Korean tradition of *Imjae Son*, which came originally from the Chinese tradition of *Linchi Ch'an (Rinzai* Zen in Japanese). This Zen tradition emphasizes the practice of questioning. These questions refer to historical cases of exchanges between a Zen master and his disciple, known as *koans.* The main point of the exchange is then taken out and used as an object of meditation, known as a *hwadu. Hwadu* literally means head of speech. It refers to that which is before any thought or word.

Linchi Ch'an, Imjae Son, and Rinzai Zen are the different pronunciation of the same Chinese characters. Although these traditions have the same name, each has evolved in its own way according to different cultural and historical circumstances. Both the Korean and the Japanese Zen traditions trace their origins back to China, but their forms today differ considerably. The Korean tradition is closer to the Chinese in the way it uses *koans.* You have the same *koan* for your whole life, and you do not generally change in midstream, even though the masters will often test you with *koans* other than your own. In your meditation practice, you always come back to the *koan* you have been given. In Japan, however, it is different. In the eighteenth century, Hakuin Zenji (1689–1769) combated a decline in Japanese Rinzai Zen by instituting a system in which you pass from one *koan* to another in a succession of tests. This system never found its way to either Korea or China. Hakuin was also responsible for the famous *koan* "What is the sound of one hand clapping?" This *koan* is not used in Korea or China.

The *hwadu* Master Kusan had told us to investigate came from a famous exchange in eighth-century China between Hui-neng, the Sixth Patriarch of the Ch'an school, and a young monk called Huai Jang (677–744). When Huai Jang came to see the patriarch for the first time, he was asked, "Where do you come from?"

Huai Jang answered, "From Mount Sung."

"What is this thing, and how did it get here?"

Huai Jang was speechless. So he stayed and practiced under Hui-neng. Eight years later, he had a breakthrough and went to be tested.

Hui-neng asked him, "What is this?"

Huai Jang replied, "To say it is like something is not to the point."

"Can it still be cultivated and experienced?"

"Although its cultivation and experiencing are not uncalled for," he answered, "it cannot be tainted."

The story of this exchange is the *koan*, and the question "What is this?" is the *hwadu*, which is singled out for meditation. Each Zen teacher has his own way to start you on this questioning. Master Kusan's way was very straightforward; you just had to ask, "What is this?" Nonetheless, I did not really know how I was supposed to do it. But, being in awe of him, I did not dare to ask for any more explanations.

So impressed was I that over the next three days I decided to become a nun. There was nothing tying me down anywhere, and the thought of living in the East had always appealed to me. Furthermore, I thought it would do me good to meditate for one or two years. Up until then I had not sat in meditation for very long nor had any idea what Buddhist nuns actually did. Nevertheless, I made up my mind and immediately told Master Kusan. He seemed pleased, and straightaway he began to consider which of his nun disciples could serve as my preceptress.

But first I had to be a postulant for at least six months, possibly a year. There was only one ordination ceremony a year. The postulancy period was to enable me to test the monastic life. Things were not made particularly easy for the postulants. We had to get up at three o'clock every morning, attend three services a day, and help in the kitchen three times a day. We needed to clean the grounds and buildings and work in the fields.

Sometimes we attended old nuns. We also had to learn several chants by heart, study basic Buddhist texts, and perform a number of bows once or twice a day. Usually I managed to find a plausible excuse to avoid the bows: there was so much work to be done in the kitchen, I was urgently needed elsewhere, or something like that.

Throughout this period we were supposed to cultivate humility and learn the basics of monastic conduct. We postulants were at the bottom of the monastic ladder, and even among us there was a pecking order. If a forty-year-old arrive a day later than an eighteen-year-old, the latter had authority over the former.

It was a hard and challenging life. Out of ten people who would arrive every month, maybe two would survive the six months to a year before becoming ordained. After the ordination, however, you were warmly received into the nunnery and distinctions of rank were made only with regard to elderly nuns and those in positions of responsibility.

For us foreigners, the situation was rather different. Because we could barely communicate, our priority was to learn the language. A nun preceptress was chosen for me a few days after Master Kusan had accepted me as a student, and it was thought best that I join her in her nunnery in Pusan, the biggest city on the southern tip of the peninsula. I was delighted to have the opportunity to stay with other nuns.

In Songgwangsa I had been given a set of nuns' clothes—a pair of baggy pants and a top buttoned down the front. So I arrived at the nunnery togged out in monastic gray but with my own colorful tee shirt and underwear beneath. But whenever I washed these few remaining Western clothes and put them on the line, they would mysteriously disappear and I would find Korean-style replacements. I was puzzled at first and looked for them all over the place. Finally it dawned on me that maybe they were being confiscated because they were inappropriate for my new life. I did not question the matter because it entailed communicating through a dictionary, a lengthy and frustrating process.

A French monk visited one day, and we talked at length about meditation. It made me think about my practice. Should I ask the question "What is it that thinks?" or "What is a thought?" I became very confused and tried to ask my preceptress, but she could not answer, which was frustrating for both of us. After two weeks, she decided to take me back to Songgwangsa to discuss these matters with Master Kusan through a translator.

In the Korean tradition one generally keeps the same *hwadu*, but as I had barely started on mine, Master Kusan decided to give me one he considered more suitable. From that point on, I was to investigate the *hwadu* "No!" The origin of this *hwadu* is as follows:

Long ago in China, Zen Master Chao-chou (778–897) gave a talk on the buddha-nature.

"The Buddha," said Chao-chou, "has ascertained that every being is endowed with the buddha-nature."

A monk pointed to a dog in the courtyard and asked: "Does this dog have the buddha-nature?"

To which Chao-chou replied: "No!"

Master Kusan instructed me to inquire deeply into this matter, to ask myself, Why did Chao-chou say "No!"? What did he mean? What was his state of mind before he said "No!"? What is this "No!"?

It took me quite some time to get the hang of this questioning. Not being an intellectual person by nature, I did not have the problem of endlessly seeking philosophical solutions, to which many Westerners are prone. But not having meditated much before, I found it very hard to concentrate on the question alone. First I spent a lot of my time daydreaming or being distracted. It was only after about three years that I started to question properly and not just repeat the question like a mantra. Finally I was able to ask with the whole of my being, so much so that sometimes my whole body and mind became a question mark. In the Zen texts it is said: "one should question with the pores of one's skin and the marrow of one's bones."

~~ The First Zen Season

A YOUNG SCOTTISH WOMAN, Anna, had also come to Songgwangsa at around that time. She had already been practicing meditation in India and Japan. Then Gudula, an older German woman, arrived. She had also been practicing in Japan and had now come to Korea for the summer season. Master Kusan had allowed them both to stay, which was very unusual, as laypeople are not supposed to join the monks and the nuns in the Zen halls during the meditation seasons. But Master Kusan had been impressed by their sincerity and made an exception. He found for them a separate room to sleep in, as well as a separate meditation hall to practice in.

A small Zen hall was created for them near the kitchen in a big room that served as an extra room for guests during the free seasons, when large parties of visitors would arrive. My preceptress and Master Kusan agreed that it would be better if I also stayed at Songgwangsa for the meditation season. I could practice with the two other Western women, work in the kitchen, and learn Korean. Whenever necessary, I could talk to Master Kusan with the help of a translator. So I joined Anna and Gudula for the summer meditation retreat. Although it was a great opportunity for me, I was rather anxious since I had never really meditated before.

A monk who had come to the monastery for the summer season was asked to be in charge and strike the wooden clapper to mark the beginning and end of the meditation periods. He kindly accepted. Two other monks who had duties in the kitchen also joined us whenever they could, plus two elderly ladies who helped in the temple. We were now eight strong and had a schedule of ten hours of meditation per day, sleeping only six hours at night.

Every morning we rose at three, attended the service in the Buddha hall, then sat in meditation until breakfast at six. We would sit for fifty minutes, practice walking meditation for ten minutes, then sit again for a further fifty minutes. The walking had two purposes: to relax the legs and get the blood circulating again as well as to get used to meditating while moving. So when the clapper was struck, we rose from our cushions and walked at a normal pace around the room, all the while maintaining a steady and vivid inquiry into the *hwadu*. I often felt my meditation was brighter, clearer, and more energetic after one of those brisk walks.

After breakfast, we sat again in meditation from seven until ten. At ten-thirty we would attend what was called the Rice Offering Service in the Buddha hall and after that have lunch. There would be further meditation from one until four in the afternoon and then we would have a little job to perform—cleaning, making a fire, and so on. At six we had a light dinner. At seven there was an evening service, after which we sat in meditation again until nine. At first these were long days.

This schedule was not unusual. It was the regular schedule for meditation halls all over the country. We were following a long tradition dating back to the eighth century, which gave a special significance to what we were doing. In regular Zen halls, instead of attending services in the morning and evening as we did, the nuns would simply bow three times in the direction of the altar on which a statue of the Buddha or a bodhisattva was placed. Or if there was a round mirror on the altar instead, they would bow to each other, as the mirror represented symbolically the reflection of everyone's buddha-nature. At the end of this brief bowing, the meditation would begin immediately.

In nunneries with Zen halls, the year is divided into "meditation seasons" *(kyolche)* and "free seasons" *(haejae)*. The former are in winter and summer, the latter in spring and autumn. Each season lasts for three lunar months. During the free seasons, the nuns may visit their home temples to pay respects to their preceptresses and elders and to help out with any work that needs to be done. Some may use the time to further their studies of the Buddhist scriptures or to chant in hermitages or temples renowned as beneficial places for chanting. Others may visit Zen masters and senior nuns for inspiration and guidance. The nuns may also travel around the country to check out different nunneries to see where they would like to stay for the following meditation season.

On the first day of a retreat, the nuns in the Zen hall have a meeting to decide on meditation and work schedules and on the various positions to be assumed during the season—who is going to be the leader, the senior adviser, tea maker, and so on. The whole assembly then comes together, and everyone announces her respective duties. These are inscribed on a long horizontal scroll, which is hung in the main dining hall for all to see until the end of the season. I always loved those big meetings where everybody was together, from the most worthy to the most lowly. The *vinaya* master would proclaim a job: "Toilet cleaner," or "fire maker," for example. A voice would pipe up out of the throng: "I'll do that." There was a very warm feeling of community, togetherness, and interdependence. Everyone was important to the well-being of everyone else.

Because I had arrived two weeks after the meditation season started, I had missed that meeting. But being a postulant I was assigned to help in the kitchen after meals and to study Korean during the free periods. The three of us, Anna, Gudula, and I, lived together in one guest room, so I used to take my textbook to the fields to enjoy the fragrance of the pine trees while reciting verbs, nouns, and phrases.

I had fun mingling with the other postulants and laywomen in the kitchen, making them laugh as I tried to communicate in my clumsy Korean. But it was less fun sitting in meditation ten hours a day. I had never done anything like it before. I had terrible pain in my back and legs and started to feel claustrophobic sitting in that one room for such long periods without moving. Even my breathing became strained. So, after the first fifty minutes of each period, I began to miss the other sitting, excusing myself on the not entirely justifiable grounds that I had to learn Korean or help in the kitchen.

Anna impressed me a lot; she could sit for hours on end without moving. And Gudula, who was supposed to be a beginner like myself, could also sit perfectly still, albeit with the help of many cushions. I, on the other hand, was terribly restless. I would be most proud of myself if I only moved half a dozen times during a fifty-minute session. My mind seemed incapable of staying still: thoughts would come and go, and if the thoughts happened to recommend learning more Korean or helping in the kitchen, then I would not resist them but would disappear for the next session to rest my tortured knees.

One day Master Kusan came to meditate with us. I diligently applied myself to my *hwadu,* moving only occasionally, but after that I could not face another hour and left. Upon my return, the monk in charge approached me, dictionary in hand. Master Kusan had asked him to tell me to *okchiro ch'amda!* We pored over the dictionary together. The words meant to bear beyond strength. I took a deep breath and promised to mend my ways. These words were among the first I learned in Korean. I never forgot them.

Despite my outward intentions, I had not really taken the activities of the Zen hall very seriously, thinking that a postulant had too many other things to do. Master Kusan, however, did take the activities of the Zen hall seriously and obviously thought that I should as well. This short episode made me reconsider my attitude, and from then on I never missed a sitting. Within a month I was even arriving early, but I was still unsure about what I was supposed to be doing. Whenever I was not distracted, which was rare, I would try to ask myself: Why did Chao-chou say "No!"? Eventually, something within me responded to the meditation, and I gradually forgot about my other interests, such as calligraphy, tai chi, and bird watching, and became absorbed in the question.

⤳ Becoming a Nun

DURING THE FOLLOWING FREE SEASON, I stayed with my preceptress for a month at her small temple in Pusan. We quickly developed mixed feelings about each other. We both had good intentions. Perhaps it was our different cultural backgrounds that kept leading to misunderstanding and unease. It was not her fault that she had been stuck with this long-nosed, round-eyed primate with puzzling behavior, whom she had to convert into a proper nun. I, a young woman with a skeptical French mind, had rebelled against authority from an early age. Yet I wanted to be a nun, so I accepted that she was my preceptress and that I had to conform. Slowly we came to terms with each other and finally learned to respect and like each other. She began to understand me while I reluctantly adapted to the norm.

She had been a devoted follower of Master Kusan for many years but because of frequent illnesses had never been able to participate in the life of the Zen hall. So, after finishing her studies of Buddhist doctrines, she had decided to serve in the small city temple founded by her own preceptress. The aims of such temples are to serve the lay community in the city. Master Kusan and other well-respected monks would visit throughout the year to give instructions and lectures. The laypeople would be encouraged to cultivate the six perfections: generosity, morality, patience, effort, concentration, and wisdom. The nuns chanted at funerals and other occasions and also counseled people whenever they faced difficulties. My preceptress's temple was also a place for postulants, generally students who had finished high school or university in Pusan, to train prior to ordination.

I had never lived in a big city before, and I did not like the place very much. I could not take long walks in the countryside and observe the subtle changes in nature. The spicy Korean food had also become a problem for me. Toward the end of the retreat at Songgwangsa, my stomach began to act up, and now it refused to get better. My preceptress took me to a doctor, where I discovered that I had gastritis.

My understanding of Korean was still poor, which led to all sorts of misunderstandings. Once my preceptress fell ill. Out of concern I went to her and said, *"Aigo chugeta. Aigo chugeta,"* believing this to mean, "I'm very sorry you are in such pain." Monks in Songgwangsa had said the same thing to me once when I had hurt myself. My preceptress gave me a funny look, and everyone else fell about laughing. I had blundered again. I went straight to the dictionary. It turned out to be a low form of speech, which should never be used toward elders, and meant something like: "Oh no! I could die!" The monks had used it in jest. As usual, I was forgiven, but I felt terribly embarrassed. In the years to come, the other nuns would remind me of this incident with great glee.

After a month I was allowed to return to Songgwangsa with two monks, disciples of Master Kusan. Before leaving Pusan, we went to Kungnagam, a small hermitage attached to the large and ancient monastery of T'ongdosa. The setting of T'ongdosa was beautiful. We walked along a path bordered by high pine trees whose canopies swayed in the breeze in a brushing murmur. The monastic buildings lay nestled in a small valley by the side of a river, which was crossed by a delicate half-moon stone bridge.

We entered the monastery and paid homage in the main Buddha hall. This hall was unusual in that it was empty of all statues. Behind the wall in front of which a statue would normally be was a reliquary reputed to contain relics of the Buddha—pieces of his robes and some *sarira* (gemlike objects sometimes found in the cremated remains of saints). Both then and on subsequent visits I always felt a great quietness and peace in that hall.

Kungnagam Hermitage was thirty minutes away, up a very steep incline, perched amidst a cluster of trees. There was a small pool in the entrance, over which stretched a stone bridge, symbolizing the crossing over to the shore of enlightenment. As usual we made our way to the main hall, where we bowed three times. Then I was taken to a room where a very ancient and frail-looking monk sat, radiating serenity. This was Master Kyongbong, one of the oldest and most venerated Zen masters in Korea. Our first exchange was very limited as I could barely communicate with him. I was impressed by his presence, and thereafter, every free season, I would go to pay my respects to him and ask for his advice.

Once when I visited him, I asked, "What should I do for the questioning to be vivid and clear?" He looked at me directly and said, "You know yourself. I have nothing to say." And he refused to say anything else. I was a little perplexed and slightly crestfallen. I wanted to get from him great words of wisdom. Then I realized what a great gift he had given me: I did not need to look outside of myself for wisdom and inspiration. I knew what to do already; all I had to do was apply it.

This truth is also pointed out in a Zen saying, "When the master raises his eyebrows or blinks his eyes, do not think he is giving instructions about the meaning of the *hwadu*." This means that basically one must trust one's own wisdom and buddha-nature and not look for an answer outside oneself. Some years later, when Master Kusan went to America, I accompanied him as a translator. On one occasion we visited a Buddhist center and met a young man who was a healer. At one point during a walk, Master Kusan brushed a fly from his cheek. The young healer stopped in his tracks and exclaimed, "Miraculous! So profound! What is the meaning of that gesture?" I dutifully turned to Master Kusan and asked him. He replied, "The fly was itching, so I just brushed it away." Sometimes we want more from reality than just plain reality itself.

During the meditation season, Anna had decided to become a nun. So there were now three Western postulants at Songgwangsa—Anna; Larry, the young American; and I. Each of us was given a Buddhist name by Master Kusan: Larry became Hyonsong, which means Dark Star; Anna became Suil, Sun of the Practice; and I became Songil, Sun of the Nature. A Buddhist name is meant to spur you along the path to enlightenment.

Back at Songgwangsa I was studying Korean assiduously as well as working hard in the fields and kitchen. We were preparing for our ordination, which was to take place in October on the commemoration day of the death of Master Kusan's teacher. There would be the three of us plus three young Korean men. At that time, in 1975, the larger monasteries would perform ordination ceremonies once a year, not only for their own postulants, but also for postulants from smaller temples nearby. Shortly afterward, the Chogye Order (the main Buddhist order in Korea, to which we belonged) decided to restore the tradition of mass ordinations. These were to be performed once a year in one of the larger monasteries by the requisite number of monks and nuns, with all the formalities stipulated in the monastic rule laid down by the Buddha. This kind of ordination would last a week and involved detailed preparations and training in the precepts to be taken. The ordination ceremony itself would last a whole day.

In contrast, the ordination we had was like a small family affair, presided over by our resident precept master. When the day arrived, we first had to have baths and shave our heads. Then we had to learn how to put on the formal butterfly-sleeved gowns and brown robes, which had been made especially for us. All six of us were both excited and apprehensive. During the ceremony we would have to kneel, our bottoms perched on our upraised ankles, for excruciating periods of time. We were warned that in this position one's legs often fell asleep, making it impossible to stand up at the required moments. I was convinced I would do something wrong.

We entered the specially prepared room. The precept master ascended the dharma platform, and we had to repeat chants and answer a baffling array of questions. I was so nervous I could barely follow the ceremony itself. All I was aware of was the physical pain of the posture and then the relief of having survived it when it was all over. Fortunately, only one of the postulants happened to get stuck in the kneeling position and failed to stand up on cue. After receiving the precepts, we thanked the assembled monks and the precept master by bowing three times. Then we went to the Hall of Avalokitesvara, the Bodhisattva of Compassion, where we performed a 108 bows as a symbol of our resolve.

We had now taken the ten precepts of a Buddhist novice. These are to refrain from: killing; stealing; sexual intercourse; lying; taking intoxicants; eating out of specified hours; using garlands or perfumes; sleeping on high beds; participating in singing, musical, or theatrical performances; and acquiring gold, silver, or jewels. These precepts made a lot of sense. It seemed clear that indulging in any of these things would not help us to develop either wisdom or compassion.

In addition to the precepts, there were eight guidelines, known as the eight heavy restrictions or special rules, for novice nuns, given by the Buddha to his foster mother when she was first admitted to the order. These guidelines are as follows:

• A nun, whatever her age, must pay proper respect to a monk, even a newly ordained monk.

• A nun must spend the summer retreat in a district where there is a monk.

• The nuns must perform the precept recitation ceremony and receive teachings on dates decided by the monks.

• The nuns perform the repentance ceremony in front of both monks and nuns at the end of the summer retreats.

• A nun who has committed an offense must confess before both assemblies, monks and nuns.

• After two years of following six precepts (which later became ten), a novice nun must be ordained by both assemblies, monks and nuns.

• A nun must never abuse a monk.

• A nun must never scold a monk but can be rebuked by a monk.

All the Buddhist traditions of Asia have these eight prescriptions for nuns. However, the way monks behave toward nuns in the different Buddhist countries varies considerably. Of all the Asian countries in which I have traveled or lived, Korean monks tend to offer the most respect to the nuns and come closest to treating them as equals. Perhaps it is different because Buddhism was repressed in Korea by the Confucian state for six hundred years. It is easier to feel equal under difficult circumstances than under opulent ones. When there is a question of survival, common humanity rather than gender is brought to the fore.

Because I did not speak Korean well, and because the monks I knew did not suddenly behave differently toward me after I was ordained, I was barely aware of the existence of these eight restrictions. When a monk and a nun of the same age and status meet, they bow to each other in the same way, both of them lowering their foreheads to the ground. Monks always return bows received from nuns and laypeople, the kind of bow only differing slightly according to age and status. Son'gyong Sunim, the venerable aged nun whose life will be recounted in the second part of this book, always made a point of bowing to young monks, but they respected her age and wisdom and would bow in return. When I finally found out about these restrictions, I was not so upset by them, because they did not seem to make any practical difference in the everyday life of the nuns.

In all my years in Korea, on only one occasion did I meet a monk who took advantage of the first restriction. He arrived one day at my preceptress's temple. He was about thirty-five and sat very straight on a high, fluffy cushion, looking important. We all bowed to the ground three times. He acknowledged us with a thin smile and a faint nod of the head. We solemnly filed out. I could not contain my surprise. A young nun pulled me aside and said with a knowing look, "He's very serious about his practice." No more was ever said.

After their ordination, Korean nuns generally enter a lecture hall *(kangwon)* for three or four years. The *kangwon* is a seminary where basic Buddhist discourses (sutras) and doctrines are studied. There are several such halls in Korea; the best known among them is Unmunsa, where over two hundred nuns study under the supervision of five nun lecturers. In the twelfth century, Unmunsa was a famous Zen monastery. However, in the following centuries it declined, although it did enjoy two periods of revival during the Confucian Choson period. After the defeat of the occupying Japanese forces in 1945 and the Korean War in the early 1950s, a nationwide reform of the Buddhist community got underway. It was at that time that Unmunsa became a nunnery and was developed into a seminary by the founding abbess, Kumkwang Sunim. I always enjoyed its beauty when I visited—the large Buddha halls and relics and the well-tended flowerbeds.

Another feature of the Korean Zen Buddhist tradition is its syncretism. It could be because Korean Buddhism suffered persecutions during the Choson Dynasty, which led to the forced mergers of a number of separate Buddhist orders. Or it could also be that because it is a small country and very group-oriented, the early Buddhist masters in Korea did not want to consider Zen meditation in isolation from studying the sutras, observing the discipline *(vinaya)*, chanting, working, or offering service to others. So a syncretic form of Zen Buddhism developed in which every aspect of the practice could be seen as a way to awaken to the buddha-nature.

In Unmunsa, as in all Buddhist lecture halls in Korea, the nuns rise at three in the morning and retire at about nine in the evening. They attend three services and practice meditation after the first service in the morning. Most of the morning and afternoon is spent in study, either in small groups or in large classes. The nuns follow a four-year course, which comprises studies of Mahayana Buddhist sutras as well as Chinese and Korean Zen texts.

As in the Zen halls, each nun has a daily task to perform and has an occasional stint in the fields. The nunnery has its own rice paddies, which provide their staple diet. Unmunsa, with its flowers and shrubs, was the neatest and prettiest temple I ever came across in Korea. It has a definite feminine touch to it. And every morning the nuns would line up to perform calisthenics in their gray attire and snowy white rubber shoes. It was quite a Buddhist sight!

At the conclusion of their studies, the nuns usually go to one of the Zen halls for nuns situated in nunneries in various parts of the country. After they have devoted themselves to the practice of meditation for a number of years, they may eventually become leaders of Zen halls or abbesses of small temples, or they may be given positions of responsibility in their home temples. It is important to remember that all nunneries in Korea operate with a high degree of autonomy and are not supervised by monks.

During much of the twentieth century, Korea suffered considerable poverty, meaning that the temples, too, were very poor. Nowadays, however, the people are much better off. When you enter a nunnery, you do not have to bring anything. You are provided with all you need for this life of simplicity and renunciation. So, by keeping the rules of conduct and thus the harmony, you can practice, study, and render service as much as you want to and can.

At the end of the meditation season, many nuns wander from temple to temple until the next season. They can stay in any temple as a guest for up to three days. Each temple gives them enough pocket money to take them to the next temple. In Korea, the ancient Buddhist tradition of monastic wandering is still very much alive. Nowadays, longer journeys are taken on the inexpensive public transport, or nuns travel by car, but in her youth Son'gyong Sunim had to walk everywhere. According to the monastic rule, nuns are expected to travel in pairs or as a small group. If during her travels a nun decides to settle in a particular nunnery, she will seek permission to do so. If she is accepted, she will then bow three times to the community of nuns in the main common room, as a formal ceremony of entry.

ᵐ Meditation in Winter

AS I COULD NOT SPEAK the language very well, there was little point in my going to a lecture hall where most of the studies required not only knowledge of Korean but of classical Chinese as well. Nonetheless, during the free season I would teach myself some Chinese characters. In that way I learned all the characters used in the daily chanting and the *Heart Sutra*. The foreign monks' and nuns' small library contained English translations of sutras and other Buddhist texts. Whenever I had the opportunity, I would study such works as the *Dhammapada*, the *Platform Sutra*, and *The Awakening of Faith*.

Because Western monks could not do the required years of study in the lecture hall like the Korean monks, an exception was made and they could join the Zen hall at Songgwangsa straight after ordination. (Nowadays the Chogye Order has tightened its procedures, and all young monks and nuns, even Westerners, have to complete their studies in the lecture hall before they can hope to join any Zen halls. Exceptions are rare.) Larry, Dark Star, did just that. For us Western nuns, it was more complex. Since we had to live separate from the monks, another place had to be found for us. This was a delicate issue. In Korea, monks stay in monasteries and nuns in nunneries. The two do not mix. Some of the monks in Songg-wangsa were therefore not keen about our staying there. However, because we were Westerners, Master Kusan compassionately persuaded them to make an exception in our case.

First we were provided with one of the guest rooms in the kitchen area, then we were moved to a room near the office, then to one next to the quarters of an old monk, then to one near the elderly laywomen who sewed for the monastery. Finally we ended up in a room in a little compound next door to the precept master. The compound, called Hwaomjon, was enclosed by a wall and had a large wooden door. Opening the door was an operation in itself. One had to put one's hand through a hole that was situated at shoulder height and then draw back a wooden bar. The door would open with an eerie creak. I loved the place; its privacy was ensured because visitors could never figure out how to open the door. In addition, we were located across the river, conveniently away from the bustle of the main monastery.

Our accommodation consisted of a single room where we meditated, studied, relaxed, and slept. We ate in the kitchen with the postulants and the lay workers who came every day from the village nearby. When we later became more numerous, our little room sometimes became rather cramped. In spite of these conditions, we were happy to have this opportunity to study under Master Kusan, an opportunity denied to Korean nuns because there was no large nunnery nearby.

As the winter meditation season approached, I toyed with the idea of going to one of the Zen halls for nuns. I was prevented, however, by a sprained ankle. Then three Western laywomen arrived from Japan. They had visited Songgwangsa in the past and had been impressed by Master Kusan, and they wanted to practice under his direction. They were all quite young, between twenty-five and thirty. There was Molly, a well-traveled American; Patricia, an American painter; and Josephina, a Swedish potter. They had all been practicing Zen in Japan at a place where Suil, formerly Anna, used to go.

The five of us barely managed to fit into the floor space at night. We did everything in that one room for the three months of the meditation retreat. The floor was warm because it was heated beneath by a system of flues, but the air was cool, the walls being made of mud and bamboo and the windows covered with rice paper. Although Josephina, from Sweden, loved fresh air, I, from the south of France, was less keen, especially at three in the morning when it was minus ten degrees Celsius outside. It was my job to light the fire beneath the room at four o'clock in the afternoon to warm the floor. The heat would last until the following morning. I enjoyed gathering twigs and logs and watching them flare up with the first match. But on a rainy day the matches would flicker out, or the logs would not burn, and then I would stink of smoke.

That winter the tap froze, and we were forced to get our water from a deep well in the courtyard. A little pail was lowered into the well with a bamboo rod. It was not an efficient method, especially as the pail would regularly detach itself and fall to the bottom of the well and one of us, generally me, had to scramble down about four meters to rescue it. But we had a wonderful meditation season. We were young, enthusiastic, and new to everything and inspired to practice diligently by Master Kusan. Considering our differences in cultures and temperament, we managed to live quite harmoniously.

In Korea, the eighth day of the last month of the lunar year is considered to be the day on which the Buddha attained enlightenment. Twenty-five hundred years ago, Gautama (the name of the Buddha before his awakening) sat under the Bodhi tree for seven days. At dawn on the eighth day, it is said, he saw the morning star and was completely awakened. To emulate this event, the nuns in Zen halls throughout Korea engage in a nonsleeping practice every year for up to a week prior to the eighth day. Like them, we decided to sit in meditation day and night, apart from eating and going to the toilet, at least for four days. This is the only time the wooden sword (a long flat stick) is used to strike meditators on the back of the shoulders when they start to nod off. Nuns and monks who were expert at these nonsleeping weeks told us that after a couple of days it became easier. I must confess that I found this lack of sleep trying, added to which it aggravated my stomach problem. After a while, though, I became so tired that I had no energy left over for distracted thoughts, or any thoughts at all for that matter. When I managed to raise the *hwadu*, however, it would come easily, and the feeling of questioning would be vivid and clear.

On the last evening of the four days, it was my turn to strike the wooden clapper that is used to signal the beginning and end of the sitting meditation. Because of my sprained ankle, I had to sit with my back against the wall and my legs stretched out. I suddenly looked down at my watch, but my brain seemed to have stopped working. I must have been asleep. I just looked at it blankly and kept sitting, but I had the nagging suspicion that an urgent message was trying to reach me through the thick fog. I picked up the watch again, but it still did not make sense to me. Finally, the mysterious message broke through, and I hurriedly struck the clapper. Everyone sighed. We had been sitting for seventy minutes, twenty minutes longer than intended. Those last twenty minutes had been sheer torment for the others who were seated in the lotus position. Afterward, we all laughed about it. But I have never sat in meditation with my back against a wall since then.

During the following free season, I took Molly and Patricia to visit some Korean nunneries before they went back to Japan. It was on this visit that I first met Son'gyong Sunim at Naewonsa, one of the renowned Zen halls for nuns. Although she was very welcoming at that time, we could not communicate very well because my Korean was still too poor. Molly and Patricia were impressed by this visit and were almost tempted to become nuns themselves.

⤳ Living with the Nuns

SUIL AND I DUTIFULLY VISITED our respective preceptresses and mutual elders (our preceptress's preceptress) at the temple in Pusan. They decided to take us in hand and make good nuns out of us. They did not think it was such a good idea for us to stay in a monastery all the time; a nun's behavior had to be learned and then refined through contact with other nuns. Since we, too, were eager to be instructed, we agreed to spend the summer with Suil's preceptress in a Zen hall called Taewonsa, located in the Chiri Mountains.

To carry our belongings from one temple to another, we were given special backpacks made of thick cotton cloth dyed with charcoal to produce the ubiquitous monastic gray. The packs look deceptively small, but they are capable of holding everything needed for a three-month retreat. We would carry two sets of ordinary gray clothes, one gray butterfly-sleeved gown, one brown patched robe (if one is fully ordained), or a small brown patched piece of cloth (to hang on one's chest from one's neck if still a novice [this is no longer in use]), four bowls wrapped in a white towel, chopsticks, spoons, underwear, socks, books, and a handful of personal belongings. We loaded the plump packs onto our backs and set off, joyful at the prospect of spending the summer meditation season with experienced nuns.

To reach Taewonsa, we had to walk the last thirty minutes on a winding dirt road along a rushing torrent. The nunnery was nestled deep in the valley, surrounded by high mountains. It was built on the site of a monastery that had been abandoned. Over the years a group of nuns had completely restored it to its former glory. The Zen hall was situated a little above the main compound, amidst a bamboo grove. It was beautiful and quiet. The life of the nuns was very simple. Living far from towns and villages, they had to be more self-sufficient and make their own tofu and acorn jelly, gather wild greens, and dig edible roots from the mountains.

That 1976 summer season with the nuns was a great challenge for me and for them, too. There were ten of us in the Zen hall. The leader was a proficient elderly nun, a hardened meditator of many seasons. She was also cantankerous, and at first I did not appreciate her at all. But throughout the meditation season I grew to like and respect her. I think fondly of her now and smile at the memory of her sitting on the veranda eating cake and telling us what was what.

Again I was faced with the challenge of having to conform to a centuries-old tradition alien to my own. I had few problems with the meditation by then, but having to work with the other nuns in the right way (theirs) was still a trial. My parents had been skeptical about my making a success of a life regimented in this way and had even written to me: "You, a nun? Never! You are too independent." I was beginning to suspect that they might be right and dreamed of escaping. Although I scrupulously followed the meditation schedule, I would often not show up or would be late for communal work or meetings, preferring to go for a walk or sit by the river instead.

But I knew all along that my conduct was out of harmony with the others, and if I really wanted to be accepted by the community, I would have to be prepared to do what was required. Meditation had become important to me; I realized that becoming a real nun was also important. So very slowly and with much effort I started to adapt. Thus I learned one of the essential rules of the Zen hall: the community does everything together, no matter what any individual might think of it. You sleep, eat, work, meditate, clean, and wash together.

As younger nuns, we were told to relieve the older nuns of their brooms immediately if we ever found them sweeping. Sometimes it sounded as though we were supposed to spend our entire time rushing in to prevent them doing anything at all. But how was I to know what their intentions were? Was I to follow them around dogging their every move? After a while I realized this was not what was meant. The point was to become more aware of what was needed. If we happened to see a lot of leaves on the path, for instance, we should remedy the situation ourselves, instead of expecting someone else to do it. This practice would help us to be more responsive to our surrounding.

Washing was one of the most important activities. Koreans as a whole are extremely clean and nuns even more so. Every evening we had to perform the four-points wash: head and armpits in the basin marked "up," lower parts and feet in the basin marked "down." Socks and shoes had to be washed every night. The shoes were made of rubber and came in black or white. Diligent nuns wore white ones. I opted for black. As they did not show the dirt, I could get away with washing them less often.

We had to sleep fully clothed apart from our gray top. In the mornings, it was a matter of putting on our shirts, splashing our faces with water, and going to our cushions. Except for a strip of cloth secured in place by a string (nuns' knickers), which we washed and changed every day, we could only change our clothes on bath day, which came around once a fortnight.

Humility and respect for the older nuns was essential. We were not supposed to look them straight in the eyes; that was considered arrogant. I also discovered that we were never to argue and should always repent when we made mistakes. This requirement was particularly difficult for us Westerners. Our first impulse was to justify ourselves with a big "but." Instead I had to learn to say, "I have made a mistake. I repent." Then everything would be forgiven and forgotten. Time after time, I was to experience this complete forgiveness.

As a Westerner, I was used to being able to talk my way out of a tight spot through the skillful use of words. Not any more—that did not work in a Korean nunnery where humility was valued more highly then cleverness. On the other hand, though, because I was now considered part of a tightly knit Buddhist family, no matter what I did, however misguided and harmful it may have been to myself or others, I was always forgiven.

Such a capacity to forgive did not come easily to me, and I was deeply moved by the nuns' ability to accept and care for each other regardless of what they had done.

Repentance could also take place in a formal way. Once without realizing it, we had been disruptive and had inconvenienced the other nuns. So, four weeks into the season, Suil's preceptress told us to go with her to the Zen hall and bow three times as an act of repentance. Our Korean was not good enough to understand why, but we did it anyway. After that we were more careful of our actions, and things went much better. By the end of the season, we had improved in the eyes of the other nuns to the point where we were almost considered proper nuns.

I had a lot of pain from gastritis that season and at one stage thought that I was going to die. At first I was filled with self-pity. Then one day I accepted the situation: my stomach was bad, so be it. This pain gave me an insight into the Buddhist first ennobling truth, that there is suffering in life. I recognized that as long as there was a body, there would be suffering. Some people had headaches, others backaches, I had a weak stomach. I should take care of it and stop indulging in self-pity. My change of attitude had a remarkable effect on the pain. Not that it went away, but it became less intense as soon as I started to identify it less as mine. The illness also made me realize what pain could be like and helped me develop more compassion for people who suffered from illness.

Korean food is very hot, large quantities of chili pepper being added to most dishes. The food in the nunneries and monasteries, however, was not so bad because no meat, onions, leeks, or garlic were ever used. This is in accordance with the bodhisattva precepts that are strictly adhered to in the preparation of food for monks and nuns. I had been a vegetarian for some years, so, apart from the chili pepper, this diet suited me well.

We had four eating bowls, each fitting neatly into the others when not being used. The biggest one was for the rice, the next one for the soup, the third one for cleaning water, and the smallest one for the side dishes. At all times we had to handle them with respect. With two hands we took them from the shelf in the main room where they were stored and put them on the floor in front of us as we sat down cross-legged on the floor. We separated them, setting them noiselessly two by two on a little mat in front of us. We then waited to be served the rice and soup. We helped ourselves to the side dishes as they were passed to us on a tray. Before eating we chanted these words:

As we receive this food
May all sentient beings including ourselves
Come to realize our true nourishment to be the happiness of
    meditation
And be filled with the joy of Dharma.
Let us reflect on our merits and recollect the source of this food.
Let us consider if our virtues are sufficient to deem us worthy of such
    offerings.
Let us protect the mind and discard error, especially greed, stupidity,
    and anger.
Food is a medicine for curing the decay of the body.
Let us take it for the purpose of perfecting our practice.

Then we would take a few grains of rice with a tiny bamboo spoon and put them into a small bowl that was passed around. After that we chanted again:

All of you spirits!
Now we give you this offering.
This food pervades the ten directions
And reaches all spirits everywhere.

At the end of the meal, these grains of rice were placed on a flat rock outside with the water used to rinse our bowls.

When everyone had eaten, warm rice water was passed around. With a firm piece of pickle speared on the end of our chopsticks, we cleaned the dirty bowls, then drank the water. The clean water that was still in the third bowl was then used to rinse the other three bowls. Next the bowls were dried and stacked together. The spoon and chopsticks were slipped into a pouch, placed on top of the bowls, then everything was wrapped in a square cloth and tied with a knot. The knot was the most delicate part of the operation; it had to be of a specific kind, look neat and tidy, and hold well. Mine always tended to work itself loose and twist awkwardly to one side.

Eating the food in this formal way made me feel quiet and light inside. There was no thought echoing in my mind from talking or thinking about the food. We just ate it carefully and mindfully—unless one of us misjudged the identity of an item of which we had accepted a generous serving. Once Suil had an extra scoop of what she thought was tomato soup. It turned out to be chili broth. Heroically she ate it all and afterward drank gallons of water.

⋙ A Silent Retreat

I WAS NOT ALTOGETHER UNHAPPY when the rigors of the summer season at Taewonsa were over, but I felt a sense of achievement and satisfaction at having done it. I was now really beginning to learn the ropes. With three months of meditation with Korean nuns under our belts, Suil and I returned to our small room at Songgwangsa. This room would be our refuge during the rest of our time in Korea, our home base, from which we could make forays into the complexities of Korean nunneries. It was a place where we could relax into our Western selves—eat porridge and buttered bread. After a while we only ate in the kitchen at lunchtime; rice and pickles three times a day was too much for us.

We decided to spend the next winter retreat in our room and keep silence. Master Kusan approved of this plan, and for the duration of the retreat the only words we ever spoke were in our interviews with him. At the beginning, this silence felt unnatural. But when I became used to it, I started to find it beneficial. With all gossip and chatter eliminated, I realized just how unnecessary most of my talking was. I felt quiet and clear. When the silent period was over, words did not come easily. Only gradually did I regain my former voice, and then it was hard to stop talking.

During that season, three young monks went to practice in a hermitage high up in the mountains, about an hour's walk away from the monastery. After a month, one of them suddenly had a deep experience of emptiness. Thinking it was enlightenment, he immediately rushed down the mountain to have his understanding checked and approved by Master Kusan.

Master Kusan hit him with his heavy wooden stick and asked him, "Do you feel pain?"

"Yes," said the monk, "that hurts!"

Master Kusan retorted, "It is not emptiness then, is it? Such experiences happen sometimes during intense practice. Go back and meditate more!"

Unconvinced, the monk stormed off to see Master Kyongbong in Kungnagam. But he received the same treatment and was again told to go back to practice more. Still unconvinced, he went to see Master Songch'ol, the patriarch of the Chogye Order, in Haeinsa. The same thing happened all over again. Finally the monk gave in, accepted the advice of the three teachers, and returned to the hermitage above Songgwangsa to resume his training.

By then both my Korean and my knowledge of Chinese characters had improved, and I could understand the daily services much better. The Homage Chant in the morning began with this invocation:

> May the sweet scent of our keeping the precepts,
> Our meditation, our wisdom, our liberation,
> And the knowledge of our liberation
> Form a bright shining cloudlike pavilion,
> Covering the whole universe
> As homage to the countless Buddhas,
> Their Dharmas and Sanghas
> In all directions.

This was followed by verses of praise to the buddhas, bodhisattvas, and masters, then it finished with these lines:

> We earnestly pray that these countless precious Ones
> Receive our devotion with love and compassion,
> Empowering us with spirituality.
> We also earnestly wish

That we and all beings in the universe
Attain buddhahood at the very same time.

I particularly liked the verse that followed, a well-wishing chant for
the whole world:

May the ocean of goodness from our practice
Return to the world to fulfill its purpose.
May the world rest in peace
And the wheel of Dharma revolve.
May each being born on this earth
Never fall back from wisdom as fierce and courageous as Buddha's.
May we attain the fruit of great awakening
And may our actions pervade the universe.
May our compassion be as vast as Lokeshvara's
And may all beings enter Nirvana.
Upon merely hearing our names, may beings avoid evil ways.
Upon merely seeing our forms, may beings attain liberation.
For innumerable aeons may we teach the Dharma,
Even though neither beings nor buddhas exist.
May the calm of this place bring an end to worry and sadness.
May all of us reach the shore of enlightenment together
And in each life practice the way of selfless service.

This chant was followed by the recitation of the *Heart Sutra,* a brief
text summarizing the Buddha's discourses on the perfection of wisdom.
The three daily services were short, not lasting more than twenty minutes.
Occasionally, there would be longer services for death ceremonies or special offering ceremonies when the *Sutra of Perfect Enlightenment* or the *Diamond Sutra,* a longer text on the perfection of wisdom, would be recited.

ᐤ Further Training

THE SEASONS ROLLED BY. Three years had passed, and I was still in Korea. During my third summer I decided to stay at Songgwangsa for the forthcoming retreat. In addition to meditating, I wanted to help in the kitchen to make up for my shorter than usual time as a postulant performing that duty. The first two months were easy enough because all I had to do was help with the side dishes and the washing up. For one week during the last month, however, life became more challenging: I was asked to take on the near-sacred duty of cooking the rice. In Korea rice is the staple diet and is usually donated to the temple by the laypeople. It is to be used wisely, and not a single grain must be wasted.

One of the basic training texts states, "From the time of ploughing and sowing until the food enters your mouth and the cotton cloth touches your body, men and oxen must suffer great pain and countless insects are injured and die." And Master Kusan used to say to us, "Are you aware of the heaviness of the four kinds of debt you are incurring? The money donated for building the temple, the food donated to feed the monks and nuns, the clothes made and given, and the medicines prescribed at times of illness? Do you fully realize how deeply in debt you are? It has been said that each grain of rice offered out of sincere faith is as heavy as Mount Sumeru."

The precept master would also frequent the kitchen to tell us how important it was not to waste even one grain of rice. We had to clean and cook enough rice to feed the whole monastery three times a day. Every time we poured the water away after washing the rice we had to be extremely careful not to let any grains of rice flow away with it. This task was an excellent training in mindfulness.

It was very important to make the rice well and in exactly the right amount. During my week as rice maker, my meditation suffered, as I spent most of my hours on the cushion calculating how many cups of rice I would have to cook for 60, 80, and, on one occasion, 120 people. So much rice! It had to be shoveled out of a big pot with a spade and a spade of cooked rice is very heavy.

Master Kusan used to tell us that we should work with our hands, but with our mind we should keep investigating the *hwadu*. During all the kitchen and field work I tried to put this advice into practice and found it very helpful. It sometimes gave me added strength. When I had to lift a big bundle of branches to load into the fire beneath the rice pot, for example, concentrating on the *hwadu* would give me the energy required. However, at the end of these three months, I was very tired. I realized that I was not ready yet to combine working full time with meditation practice. So for the next three years I decided to devote myself strictly to Zen training.

I decided to spend the following meditation season under the direction of Master Songdam, the Zen master of Yonhwasa, a small temple in the port of Inchon, near Seoul. As a young monk, Master Songdam had kept silence for ten years, talking only at night to his teacher. After he gained insight, he worked on a project to reclaim land, as a way to test and strengthen his understanding. At fifty he was younger than most Zen masters, and I found his teachings clear and inspiring.

Although there was a Zen hall for laywomen in Yonhwasa, because it was a monastery they would not accept nuns. However, Master Songdam used to go to the city of Taejon to teach at a Zen hall for nuns there. I tried several times to enter this hall, but it was popular and always fully booked years in advance. I managed to find another Zen hall at P'alchongsa, a nunnery in the hills near the center of Seoul. The Zen hall was built in the upper story of a concrete building. In front of it stood an ancient temple, and from the large bay window of the hall one could contemplate the ancient crenellated wall of the old city snaking along the hills. The wall seemed to be protecting the city from nothing more threatening than elegant pine trees sprinkled in snow. Sitting in the Zen hall, the nuns needed not have any sense at all of the six million people crowded into the city around them.

Five of us occupied the Zen hall. There were two senior nuns, both over fifty, who had spent many seasons in different Zen halls. They had recently had some health problems, which made it difficult for them to join a larger hall. In P'alchongsa, the schedule was not as rigorous and the atmosphere was more informal. One younger nun had come to help with the retreat, and the leader, Songou Sunim, was a veteran nun of about forty.

I was impressed by Songou Sunim. She seemed always free of cares and clear-headed. Whenever I made a mistake, she would know how to explain in a kind way what the matter was. She had been a nun for many years, practicing Zen for at least twenty of them. At some point in the past, she had decided to meditate without depending on anything. She even stopped sitting on a cushion. I tried to follow her example but found it painful on my back, so I quickly renounced this act of renunciation. Songou Sunim had studied for many years under one of the greatest nun Zen masters of the last century, Mansong Sunim. During the tea break, she would tell us stories about Mansong Sunim and how she used to teach with both great understanding and severity.

During the retreat we were able to attend the dharma talks that Master Songdam gave every fortnight at his temple in Inchon. Whenever he told us to penetrate into "What is this?" or "No!" I felt a deep sense of inquiry arising in me. In private interviews his presence was very powerful, making all distracted thoughts disappear and the questioning become very vivid. He advised me to practice the *hwadu* while concentrating on my breathing. I was to breathe in, hold the breath for a moment, then as I breathed out, ask, "Why did Chao-chou say 'No!'?" I tried this technique for a while, but my lungs quickly became congested and breathing difficult. When I told him that, he advised me to drop this method. A few months later, however, I tried it again. I found that whenever my concentration and inquiry were clear and vivid, this method would come naturally.

Being of a younger generation, Master Songdam had many lay disciples, and his approach was quite modern. I sometimes had the chance to observe exchanges he had with laypeople. One woman was worried about her son, who was intensely shy and overweight. Master Songdam told her to feed him nothing but brown rice, vegetables, and fruit for one month. Within that time, the boy became visibly thinner and also less fearful. After several months on this diet, he lost all his excess weight and became quite friendly and outgoing. On another occasion, an old lady was troubled about her son, who was very aggressive and violent. Master Songdam advised her to talk to him about love and kindness in his sleep.

My domestic responsibility for the duration of the retreat was to clean the communal bathroom. I would do this chore at four o'clock every afternoon. At the very same time, though, another nun would appear and proceed to wash herself before performing an afternoon ceremony at which she had to officiate. This went on for several weeks and I began to feel extremely resentful. Then one day I went down at four o'clock, and it suddenly didn't matter any more that she was there washing herself. It was my time to clean and her time to wash. How wonderful it felt to be free of resentment! Although a small incident, it was somehow very meaningful to me. It showed that meditation worked quietly. Without my intentionally forcing any changes, it dissolved the grasping and attachments that gave rise to the irritation.

During this retreat at P'alchongsa I had to confront a certain spiritual crisis. At the Lunar New Year in mid-February, we had to perform a special ceremony I had never encountered before. We stood outside on the steps of the Buddha hall in the cold, next to open sacks of rice. Lodged in the rice were candles, which laypeople would come up to light and then give donations. In exchange they would receive incantations written on pieces of paper, which they kept as amulets. The donors believed the incantations would bring them good fortune for the coming year. Meanwhile we chanted, invoking various spirits and gods.

I was deeply concerned because for me, Buddhism was about self-reliance without dependence on any gods. After the ceremony, I reflected on the teaching that had inspired me in the past. I realized how important meditation was in the development of compassion and clarity, and how the basis of meditation was the cultivation of morality, concentration, and wisdom. Finally I calmed down and told myself that although this ceremony was important for the lay supporters, it only played a minor role in the life of the nuns. So I decided not to let it deflect me from Zen practice. I then renewed my commitment to the Buddha, Dharma, and Sangha. Later I understood that these ceremonies took place in small temples and were performed in response to the religious beliefs of laypeople and also to help the finances of temples who had fewer resources.

In fact these ceremonies are simply another sign of the syncretic nature of Korean Zen Buddhism. When Buddhism came to Korea, the monks did not reject the local gods and spirits but skillfully incorporated them into the tradition. People were not discouraged from worshiping them but taught that such prayers to an external deity were not an end in themselves, as they needed to take further steps toward realizing the buddha-nature within themselves.

⟿ Soldiers and Apple Pie

MASTER SONGDAM'S TALKS inspired me so much that I visited him every free season for the next seven years. I also made up my mind to spend the following winter season near his temple. This time I found a place in a nunnery called Huiryongsa, a Zen hall situated on the outskirts of Seoul, high in mountains strewn with giant white boulders.

The abbess of the nunnery was an elderly nun of seventy, committed to meditation practice, who had created an active Zen hall. She was very frail but had great determination. She had managed to inspire a group of sincere laypeople to support ten to fifteen nuns for the duration of the biannual meditation seasons. She was helped by her main disciple, who had taken charge of the administrative work of the nunnery. This disciple was in her mid-fifties, very efficient, compassionate, and socially aware. In addition to supporting the nunnery, she had raised funds for a nearby school for poor children. She was also very active in helping soldiers and Buddhist chaplains in the army.

We were only sixty kilometers away from the Demilitarized Zone, a stretch of no-man's-land separating North and South Korea. It was a tense area where violent incidents would often flare up since only an armistice, rather than a peace treaty, had been signed in 1954 at the end of the Korean War. On my walks I would sometimes find brightly colored propaganda leaflets lying on the ground that had been carried across by balloons. They would tell of how pleasant it was across the border in North Korea and how sensible it would be to defect there. Once during our retreat the administrator-nun asked me whether I would like to accompany her on a visit to an army camp stationed near the Demilitarized

43

Zone. I was interested in going because living in South Korea, one could not but be aware of the tensions between North and South Korea, so we went.

We drove to the first military base, loaded down with boxes of fruit and biscuits. There we changed vehicles and went by jeep to a number of outposts, leaving some of the fruits and biscuits with the Buddhist chaplain to distribute later. We even went as far as the South Korean side of the Demilitarized Zone to take a close look at the other side, that is, North Korea. The whole thing was quite frightening. Grave, unsmiling sentries were posted every fifty meters, and they stared across at us. A fearful sense of war came over me, something I had never encountered before.

The day ended with our assisting at a Buddhist ceremony in a football field. Two hundred soldiers listened to a dharma discourse and then solemnly took the five precepts, vowing not to kill, steal, have wrongful sexual intercourse, lie, or drink alcohol. Being young soldiers, I wondered how they would be able to keep these precepts. The Buddhist chaplain felt that it was important to give these young men a sense of morality and plant a seed of dharma in their minds.

As a preliminary act of purification before formally taking the precepts, a small piece of wick was placed on the inside of the left forearm of each man and then lit. I helped put the wicks on their arms and light them. It was strange to see these tough men wince from something that actually gave very little pain. The whole day had a surreal quality to it.

During that winter, I tried hard to put all my energy into meditation. The schedule included ten hours of meditation a day, but I made a point of sitting during the free time as well, sometimes managing to sit as much as sixteen hours a day. No matter how hard I tried to maintain my inquiry into the *hwadu*, however, thoughts would still burst through to distract me, and then refuse to go away, like some insidious illness.

During one particularly bad period, no matter how hard I tried I was unable to raise the *hwadu* for two whole weeks and was besieged with nothing but wandering thoughts, daydreams, and drowsiness. Then one day we listened to the recording of a talk by Master Songdam's teacher. He simply said how important it was to raise the *hwadu,* seize hold of it, and question with the energy and single-mindedness of one's entire being. This talk gave me renewed determination. When I next sat, I almost immediately seized hold of the *hwadu* and questioned deeply. From then on, my inquiry was vivid and clear again.

I realized that questioning was not an intellectual exercise but a total body and mind experience. An analogy came to mind. If you have a child from a Pacific island who has never seen snow, you can talk to her about snow, but she will not really know what it is. If you take her near snow and show it to her from far away, she will get a better idea, but still she will not know. But if you take her to the snow, she can jump in it, touch it, and taste it. Only then will she have a total experience of snow. In the same way, I found that in the questioning itself, there was the tasting.

I also discovered that coming back to the question brought me vividly back to the present. Awareness of the question was not separate from a wide-open awareness, which neither grasped nor rejected anything. The more I would question, the more quietness and clarity would arise. At the same time, I would not only become more aware of my surroundings but also of myself and others. This awareness helped me to see myself and others more clearly, which in turn helped me to accept myself and others more compassionately and wisely.

Master Kusan always used to tell us not to succumb to confused states of mind. If the practice did not go well, we should not be sad, and if the practice went well, there was no reason to be especially joyful. He emphasized the cultivation of patience and endurance. These qualities would then help us develop tranquility and inquiry.

In one of the private interviews I had with Master Songdam, I told him about the difficulty I was having with daydreams. He said, "I'll take care of that." He then took hold of a flat wooden stick, generally used for waking people dozing in meditation, and tapped me with it on one shoulder. As he did this, he said, "From now on you will have no further daydreams in meditation." Strangely enough, for the next year I didn't have a single daydream! Occasionally distracted thoughts would bother me, but not a single daydream entrapped me.

One of the nuns in our Zen hall could not sleep at night because of a strange affliction she had. Quite unintentionally and unpredictably, an explosion would burst from her mouth like a gunshot. It was very trying for the leader of the hall when it would happen during meditation. The first time I heard it, I nearly jumped off my cushion, wondering what on earth it was and where it came from. Afterward, during the rest periods, she would then chatter nonstop in the tea room.

In her early days as a nun, she had tried to meditate too hard and in the wrong way. As a result, the nuns explained, energy had accumulated in her head and made her ill. It was a phenomenon they called *sanggi* (rising *chi*). I was told she had gotten much better. Strangely, it was because I had heard of that nun that I had chosen to come to this nunnery. She was really quite a character and loved telling bizarre Zen stories. She was rather large and tall for a Korean and stood out among the ordinary diminutive Korean nuns. I had mixed feelings about her, though. I admired her strength and dedication, but I was worried about her talkativeness. Zen stories are fun, but to listen to someone tell them compulsively is a strange experience.

That winter we chose to spend only four days commemorating the Buddha's enlightenment with extra hard practice. We opted to sleep for only three hours a night and, except for eating, would sit in meditation for the rest of the time. Although I found this easier than not sleeping at all, the effect was much the same. Distracted thoughts ceased because of my tiredness, and by the end of the four days the *hwadu* was very vivid, leaving just a state of clear, calm questioning in the midst of deep quiescence.

Shortly before the end of the season, the old leader had her birthday. To celebrate this occasion, I decided to cook the nuns an apple pie. By chance we had all the ingredients, and I figured I could use the dying embers of the fire that heated the floor as a makeshift oven. It was not exactly perfect, but it worked surprisingly well. I was rather pleased with myself as I presented a piece of my pie to the leader. She thanked me profusely. Then I said that I would like to offer the remaining pieces to the other nuns in the main dining room. To my surprise, they all said they had pressing duties to attend to and disappeared before they even had a chance to touch the pie. I was baffled. But then I looked at my creation through my newly developing Korean eyes and realized how very uninviting it must have been to them—a slab of hard dough topped with singed slices of apple. In those days, Koreans did not have ovens and did not make pastry or cook fruits. After this episode, I refrained from displaying my culinary skills.

Not long after that season, I met a monk from Songgwangsa in Seoul. When he asked me how the meditation season had gone, I replied, "Very well indeed. I think I practiced the hardest of them all!" He looked at me coldly and said, "Don't you think that's a rather presumptuous claim to make?" His response shocked me. I had thought I was better than the others because I had sat more and talked less. I suddenly realized that those things in themselves did not presuppose any great wisdom or insight. My remark had been judgmental and ego-centered.

Later an Australian monk came to Songgwangsa to study, and in the free season I took him to meet an old Zen master I knew who lived an unassuming existence in a small temple in the suburbs of Seoul. I was slightly apprehensive because I knew the Australian to be rather full of himself and critical of others. True to form, he asked the old man, "What should we do about all these monks who do not practice seriously enough?" The master said, "Let me tell you a story. There was once a Zen master who had two disciples. One would meditate with his back as straight as a rod and his eyes bright and shining, the other with his back bowed and his head lolling on his chest. One day the Zen master said to the sloucher, 'Just look at him over there; he always sits upright, full of determination, and meditates keenly. You should take him as an example! Go on, straighten your back and meditate as he does!' Then the Zen master whispered to the other disciple, 'Just look at him over there. He's not as full of himself as you are. His meditation is so deep that he forgets his own body and enters into deep concentration as soon as he sits down. You should really take him as your example!' "

In Korean Zen there is not a strong emphasis on formal posture. You are encouraged to sit upright with your back straight but in a relaxed way. Sharpness of mind is considered the most important—to keep the *hwadu* vivid and clear within a deep quietness at all times.

∼ Living with Son'gyong Sunim

IN AUTUMN 1979 I decided to apply to enter Naewonsa, a nunnery near Pusan with a large Zen hall, which I had visited some years before. Their Zen hall was so popular that it was always fully booked during the meditation season with about seventy nuns. During the free season, however, most nuns left to travel and attend to other affairs, while a few would stay, sitting a less-demanding schedule. To my delight, they let me spend a month there during the free season.

It was during this stay that I got to know Son'gyong Sunim, whom I had briefly met on my first visit. By that time my Korean had improved enough to be able to converse easily with her. We immediately hit it off, and I spent most of my free time with her, listening to her advice and the account of her experiences as a nun for sixty years.

There were about twenty of us in the Zen hall. We would sit in meditation eight to ten hours a day. At night we would simply take quilts from the wall cupboards, spread them out on our respective spots, and go to sleep. When the bell rang at three o'clock the next morning, we'd roll them up and exchange them for our meditation cushions. Then we would go outside to the toilet and wash our faces. On returning to the hall we would don our ceremonial robes, bow three times to the statue of Manjusri seated behind glass on the altar, fold our robes over the horizontal bamboo poles suspended from the ceiling, and then take our places on our cushions. The hall leader would strike the wooden clapper three times, and the formal meditation would begin. And all this would be accomplished in a very companionable silence.

In the early morning and evening we would sit facing each other to discourage dozing; during the day we would sit with our backs to each other facing the wall. As my rank (in terms of years as a nun) was very low, I found myself sitting opposite Son'gyong Sunim across this large Zen hall. When I glanced at her in the early morning, I noticed that as soon as she hit the wooden clapper, her head would drop and she would seem to fall fast asleep. Toward the end of the fifty minutes, I started to worry, "My knees are hurting . . . I hope she wakes up on time." But invariably, a few minutes before having to hit the clapper, she would straighten up, very bright and clear, and strike it on the dot. This never failed to amaze me. At lunchtime, after a short service in the Buddha hall, we ate formally in the Zen hall in the meditation posture.

Sometimes we would do common work such as sweeping the courtyard or tending the fields. One of our tasks was to gather acorns to make jelly. We would first pick a vast amount of acorns. These were then beaten to powder and sifted into fine flour, which was put into a cloth inside a large tub. For several days it would be soaked in water, the water being changed daily. The final batch of water was kept and poured into a large cauldron. An ingredient was added to thicken it, and the mixture was then heated. When it was cold, it set into a brown jelly, which was cut into small cubes to be eaten with soya sauce. Unfortunately it was rather tasteless. Son'gyong Sunim could have rested because of her old age, but she was always the first one to go to work, and during the free time she would always gather more acorns. I would often join her, as it was so enjoyable working alongside her. She unfailingly radiated kindness, peace, and joy.

Zen Master Hyanggok lived in a temple near Pusan and often came to Naewonsa to give dharma talks. He often said that nuns were more serious than monks, and he devoted a lot of time to them. He was very tall and imposing, with a great booming voice.

One day I went with a few nuns to help at a special ceremony being held at Master Hyanggok's temple. After the ceremony we had the opportunity to talk with him. He asked me how my meditation was going. I said, "So-so." Then he declared in his booming voice, "It is because you are dark, very dark, so dark; burdened by the darkness of ignorance. You must practice hard and investigate deeply, then the veil of darkness will lift."

I was left perplexed by this remark. What did he mean? I did not feel so very dark—confused perhaps. Then I saw that in a way it was true; I was clouded by a fog of ignorance. Whenever the questioning was vivid and the awareness bright, my thoughts, actions, and feelings would appear clearly. In that state I experienced peace and understanding. No longer did I feel isolated from the world but in harmony with it. When the sun shines, everything is clear and sharp. Whereas when I was lost in daydreams, fantasies, ruminations, and obsessions, everything became sticky and opaque, like when the sun is covered by thick clouds for many days.

I appreciated very much my time at Naewonsa. We were able to be ourselves while at the same time living harmoniously together. It was there that I received my greatest compliment when a nun told me that although I was a Westerner, I knew how to behave properly in the Zen hall. She implied that I knew how to take care of myself without bothering anyone else, as well as how to consider the needs of the community. When I left after a month, I felt greatly enriched by the experience.

I maintained this special connection with Naewonsa, and every free season for my remaining five years in Korea I would visit this nunnery and pay my respects to Son'gyong Sunim. As a female teacher, she was quite different from Master Kusan. She did not give dharma talks as such—she taught more by example. Whenever the nuns asked for her advice with some problems or difficulties, her recommendations were always considerate and very practical, taking into consideration the whole community of nuns. Although I tried my best to spend a meditation season there, I was always too late in applying and never managed to secure a place. In 1980, thirty nuns started a three-year retreat in silence. During the meditation season, other nuns would join them in their very strict schedule.

During the free season the thirty would go on in silence, with a lighter meditation schedule of ten hours a day. Although they were in silence, there was such a joy and warmth about them that whenever I visited during that period, I felt as though I had entered paradise. The atmosphere was spiritually charged, but also light and friendly.

A Visit Home

AFTER I HAD BEEN in Korea for nearly five years, I received a letter from my family in France saying that my father was not well. I decided to go home for a while. On my way I stopped in Taiwan to visit the nunnery of a Chinese nun I had met some years before in Seoul at a Buddhist conference. Her name was Venerable Shig Hiu Wan. She was a painter, scholar, and meditation teacher. She was exceedingly bright and energetic for her seventy-five years.

While in Korea she had met Master Kusan. They had the following exchange:

> Ven. Shig Hiu Wan: Thought comes from nonabiding.
>
> Master Kusan: What is nonabiding?
>
> Hiu Wan: Do not adhere to existence or nonexistence, and do not stand in the middle either!
>
> Kusan: So what is that which arises before thinking?
>
> Hiu Wan: The arising is nonexistence. Hence it is called wonderful existence.
>
> Kusan: "Wonderful" is only a word. Say something more before this one word.
>
> Hiu Wan: If there is one word which can be talked about, it is no word.
>
> Kusan: How do you use no-word? Within this or apart from this?
>
> Hiu Wan: When you use it, you just use it. It is like the moon moving without a trace.

Kusan: I did not ask about the moon without a trace. What is the mind?

Hiu Wan: The mind is originally nothing, so there is no word that can answer. Please be compassionate, Venerable One!

Kusan (laughing): The clouds disperse over a thousand miles and the moon shines alone.

Ven. Shig Hiu Wan belonged to the T'ien-t'ai tradition, a syncretic school of Buddhism founded in sixth-century China. In addition to her nunnery, she also directed a Buddhist institute for laywomen and nuns. Here the students practiced meditation, recited chants, studied Buddhist scriptures, learned languages, and also did painting and calligraphy. It was interesting for me to be in a different Buddhist environment and to see what was common and what was different from Korea. Before sitting in meditation, for example, we would walk very fast in the hall for up to thirty minutes. Ven. Shig Hiu Wan was an advocate of fast walking as a counterbalance for long sittings.

I stayed in France for five months and watched my father's health slowly deteriorate. Then one morning as I sat with him, I watched him take his last breath. The full impact of impermanence was brought home to me at that moment. Here was a corpse, but it looked still so alive, as if it were still breathing. I realized in my whole being that we can die at any moment, that we stand very close to death all the time. It made me want to cherish the world, truly love it. It was very sad to see my father die, but I was grateful for having been present during those last few months of his life.

On my return to Korea, I found that only two Western nuns remained at Songgwangsa. Anna had left, as well as all the Western monks. Moreover, the two nuns had gone off to practice in a nunnery for the winter season. Nevertheless, I found a great pile of mail waiting for the foreign Sangha. People from around the world were beginning to hear of Master Kusan, and some of them were keen to join the monastic and meditative life of Songgwangsa. Within three years, we were to be a community of fifteen foreign monks and nuns.

I had planned to practice meditation at the nunnery of Kyongsongam Hermitage, but it was suggested that it might be better for me to stay and practice under the guidance of Master Kusan. In this way another aspect of the nun's life presented itself to me: service. I was to become the link between the foreigners and the Koreans, working as secretary to Master Kusan and as translator for the other foreign monks and nuns who could not speak Korean.

In Korea at that time, Songgwangsa was the only established place where foreign monks and nuns could live and train. Its growing reputation meant that we were regularly visited by foreigners, tourists as well as people with an interest in Buddhism. It was my responsibility to teach them proper etiquette while they were staying at the temple. I often had to anticipate difficulties that might arise from cultural differences. One case I failed to anticipate concerned a young Israeli who was staying overnight. I showed him to his room and told him that breakfast was at six o'clock. At six I went to his room to see if everything was all right. I knocked and opened the door to find him eating away in nothing but underwear. I had to get him clothed as quickly as possible before any monks came by to chat with him. But he seemed perfectly happy as he was and failed to take my hints about putting on more clothes. He explained that he was very comfortable because the room was so lovely and warm. At that moment the former abbot, an elderly and venerable monk, arrived to practice his English on our foreign guest. I was alarmed. Luckily the monk took it very well, but as soon as he left, I had to tell the young man firmly that in a Buddhist temple one had to wear one's clothes at all times.

Often Western students of Japanese Zen Buddhism would come to visit, and I would translate during their interviews with Master Kusan. He would try to check their understanding, asking them, "What is it?" Some of them would push a cup toward him or babble or give a shout. Then he would ask, "Before you move the cup, before you babble, before you shout—What is it?" None of them could answer. It seemed that he was trying to direct them toward the essence of things rather than remaining caught up in traditional gestures and responses.

Sometimes I was called upon to translate between the foreign monks and the Korean monks when there was a misunderstanding or if a new policy or schedule had to be explained. Once we had an old German monk who was very sincere but also very stubborn and argumentative. Because he was only a novice monk of one year's standing, he had to pay proper respect to all the other monks, including a senior Korean monk who lived in the same compound and tended to talk a lot while the other monks were meditating. This habit made the German very angry, and finally he could contain himself no longer and yelled at the elder Korean to shut up. I was called in great haste. Mayhem was about to break loose. Everybody was gathered together. The Koreans emphasized very strongly that to maintain harmony in the community, everybody had to know his place and should respect the senior monks with the humility that was due to them. The German monk was embarrassed about having created such a furor and promised, albeit reluctantly, never to do it again. Fortunately, he kept his word.

✎ Advice from Master Kusan

THE GERMAN MONK tried very hard in his practice of the *hwadu*. Once while we were on our way to the fields to work, I was waiting with him and Master Kusan for some tools to arrive. The German monk took the opportunity to tell Master Kusan of his difficulties in keeping the *hwadu*, especially when working. Master Kusan said that for himself, he was able to maintain the *hwadu* all the time. The German monk exclaimed, "But why should you need to work on a *hwadu* once you are enlightened?" Master Kusan said, "As the practice evolves, the *hwadu* also evolves. I still use a *hwadu* but in a different way." The German monk asked him how he did it now as opposed to before. But the master refused to reply, pointing out that any explanation would be meaningless, and concepts about it would only be a hindrance to real inquiry.

During one season Master Kusan explained to the postulants one of the basic texts for novices, which was chanted at three o'clock every morning to the accompaniment of a wooden bell to rouse the community at Songgwangsa. As the foreign postulants wanted to attend, I had to translate for them. The text is made up of three parts. The first, *Advice for Beginners on the Way,* by Master Puril Pojo (the founder of Songgwangsa), opens with these words:

A beginning mind should keep away from bad company and draw near the virtuous and wise. When you receive the five or ten precepts, you should learn when to keep them and when to occasionally overlook them. From now on you should depend solely upon the words of the Buddha and pay no heed to the senseless comments of ordinary men.

The second text, *On Cultivating Determination to Practice*, by Master Wonhyo (617–686), adds:

Now, all the Buddhas adorn the palace of tranquil extinction (of nirvana) because they have renounced desires and practiced austerities on the sea of numerous *kalpas*. All sentient beings whirl through the door of the burning house (of *samsara*) because they have not renounced craving and sensuality during lifetimes without measure. Though the heavenly mansions are unobstructed, few are those who go there; for people take the three poisons (greed, hatred, and delusion) as their family wealth. Though no one entices others to evil destinies (animals, hungry ghosts, and denizens of hell), many are those who go there; for people consider the four snakes (the four elements of earth, air, fire, and water) and the five desires (wealth, sex, food, fame, and sleep) to be precious to their deluded minds.

Who among human beings would not wish to enter the mountains and cultivate the path? But fettered by lust and desires, no one proceeds. But even though people do not return to mountain fastness to cultivate the mind, as far as they are able they should not abandon wholesome practices.

The last text, *On Self-Admonition* by Master Yaun, lists ten guidelines to help the novices in the everyday life of the temple. The first one reads:

Beware of accepting soft clothes and fine foods.
How can you endure the thought that others have suffered through hard work in order that you can live? How can you who have an easy life complain of hunger and cold when the farmer is

also hungry and cold and the weaving woman is insufficiently clothed? A very heavy debt is incurred through wearing fine clothes and eating fine foods. Such a debt becomes a hindrance to your practice. Yet the debt incurred through wearing ragged clothing and eating only vegetables is light and will not prevent the accumulation of virtue. Remember, if you fail to awaken during this life, you may be unable even to swallow a drop of water in the next. As a verse says:

When hungry, eat roots and berries.
When naked, wear garments of pine-thread, grass, and leaves.
When lonely, befriend the wild birds and the clouds.

Thus pass your life in high mountains and deep valleys.

At the end of the study session the Western novices would ask Master Kusan questions.

Q: How can a beginner practice diligently in the face of many interruptions?

A: One's practice becomes even better when one makes an effort to keep the *hwadu* vivid in trying circumstances. Just sitting quietly will not ensure that the practice will progress. One should learn to practice while working and in the midst of difficulties. One does not meditate with the hands or the feet, but inside oneself. As long as one does not let go of the *hwadu,* the practice will progress. All practitioners have had to meditate in difficult circumstances; none have practiced in comfort and ease.

Q: Is it necessary to develop faith in order to practice meditation?

A: Yes. If one has no faith, one cannot practice successfully. To have faith is to have the firm conviction of the effectiveness of meditation practice.

Q: In your own case, did your degree of faith always remain the same or did it change with time?

A: There were certainly times when my faith was stronger and times when it was weaker. There were certain times when I was practicing on Mount Kaya, Mount Chiri, and in Sudo Hermitage when I put everything into the practice and did not care whether I lived or died. I was completely unaware of the passing of time. I once spent seven days continuously standing in meditation without ever lying down. At these times one should rest for a while before putting all one's effort into the practice again.

Q: So what is the relationship between faith and practice?

A: There is true faith and true practice. The beginner should think: I must attain buddhahood through awakening to the mind; I must cease to do evil and only do good. But a mature practitioner lets go of all such thoughts.

Q: Does one's faith become the doubt?

A: Yes. The doubt which gathers in a brilliant mass is also faith.

Q: Why is it so difficult to realize the Way?

A: Because you do not allow your mind to rest and let go of things. For this reason you cannot awaken. The Way is not easy because you do not lay down your mind. To search for the Way, to try to become Buddha, these are obstacles to the Way.

Q: But why is it still difficult to realize the Way even when one's faith and determination are strong?

A: Although you have given rise to faith, you must do so completely and thoroughly. But so far, the roots have not yet fallen away. Therefore, you cannot realize the Way. For "the roots to fall away" means that through the practice of meditation, the body as well as the universe must be experienced as empty. From this place of emptiness, the Way springs forth.

Q: How can one meditate while working?

A: Meditation is not just a matter of sitting. While working you should continue diligently to investigate "What is this?" This is meditation. When the ancients were engaged in work, internally they were always meditating. Therefore, they came to awaken upon hearing the call of a bird flying through the air or upon seeing a flower in bloom. Sitting by itself is not meditation. And when you are working with someone else, you should neither try to become especially friendly nor long for quiet by withdrawing into yourself. Someone who can work in this way is truly practicing meditation. No matter what activity you are doing, hold firmly to the *hwadu* and sustain your questioning. Then the *hwadu* and the work will become a single mass. Once they have coalesced in such a way, awakening can happen.

～ Adding Feet to the Snake

I WAS ALSO THE TRANSLATOR during the meditation season for the fortnightly dharma lecture. After some chants and silent meditation, Master Kusan would ascend the dharma platform, hit it three times with a wooden stick, and start speaking. The first part of his lecture would always be very elevated and paradoxical, and few people understood it. It would go like this:

> With one step you can cross the entire universe. There is nothing lacking and nothing superfluous. All of you gathered here today, have you awakened to this thing? If you have realized it, say something! Truly what is it like?

Rarely would anyone answer. The master would then take hold of his staff, strike it hard on the base of the dharma platform, and say, "This single staff extends above the three worlds and pervades the universe throughout the ten directions! Do you understand?"

After a period of silence he would sing a verse with an undulating voice:

> When one blade of grass leans over, the whole universe leans with it.
> All the worlds throughout the ten directions are contained in a single mustard seed.
> Enlightenment is already realized in the initial determination.
> The attainment of nondiscrimination is already present in earnest meditation.

After these direct statements, he would say that he would "add some feet to the snake," that is, explain something to us in terms we could understand. He might tell us about the ten diseases one had to avoid in *hwadu* practice, which are:

• Do not entertain thoughts of "is" or "is not," "has" or "has not."

• Do not think that Chao-chou said "No!" because in reality there is just nothing.

• Do not resort to principles or theories.

• Do not try to resolve the *hwadu* by making it an object of intellectual inquiry.

• When the master raises his eyebrows or blinks his eyes, do not take such things for indications about the meaning of dharma.

• Do not regard the skillful use of words as a means to express the truth.

• Do not confuse a state of vacuity and ease for realization of the truth.

• Do not take the place where you become aware of sense-objects to be the mind.

• Do not just rely on words quoted from the teachings.

• Do not just remain in a deluded state waiting for enlightenment to happen.

At other times he would explain in detail the sixteen conducts one had to cultivate to help one's meditation. These are presented in the form of sixteen questions:

• Are you aware of the heaviness of the four kinds of debt you are incurring?

• Are you aware that with the passing of each thought, this impure body composed of the four elements is decaying?

• Do you realize that your life force depends upon each single breath?

• In this lifetime have you met the buddhas and patriarchs?

• When you hear a discourse on the unsurpassable dharma, do you appreciate how rare and precious such an occasion is?

• Do you stay within the monastery grounds and observe your moral precepts?

• Do you engage in unnecessary conversation with those who sit next to you?

• Do you incessantly create agitation by provoking arguments?

• Is your *hwadu* bright, clear, and uninterrupted throughout the twenty-four hours of the day?

• Does your *hwadu* remain continuous and unbroken even during conversations?

• In the face of adverse and favorable conditions, do your perceptions of seeing, hearing, feeling, and so on form a single mass?

• When reflecting on yourself, are you confident that you will be able to surpass the buddhas and patriarchs?

• Are you confident that during this lifetime the wisdom of the Buddha will be definitely transmitted to you?

• While your body is healthy and you are still able to go where you wish and sit in meditation, do you reflect on the sufferings of hell?

• With this body that is the fruition of past actions, will you be able to liberate yourself from endless transmigration within the cycle of birth and death?

• Does your mind remain unmoved when subjected to the eight winds?

Often Master Kusan would give examples. He would tell us to practice as urgently as if trying to extinguish fires on our heads. In such circumstances we would not stop to think or ask questions, we would just do everything to put out the fire. Or he would encourage us to practice morality, concentration, and wisdom like a hen hatching eggs. When a hen is hatching her eggs, she moves them about with her feet so that the heat is evenly distributed. In the same way, we should practice in such a way that morality, concentration, and wisdom are evenly balanced in our lives.

He would also refer to the seasonal conditions around us. In winter he would talk about the ice in the frozen river: "If the sun shines for one day but does not for the next three days, the ice will not melt. But if the sun shines continuously for several days, the ice will melt and the water can be used for many purposes. In the same way, you should practice continuously and not in fits and starts."

At other times he would use things in the room as examples. He would hit his wooden staff on the platform and ask, "Do you hear this?" Then he would hold it up. "Do you see this? What is it that hears and sees?" Or he would turn to the clock in the room (all Zen halls in Korea had noisy mechanical clocks on their walls, which Westerners found annoying but Koreans refused to have removed) and say, "Look at this clock. Hear its teaching on the dharma! With each tick-tock you are approaching death. Time is always running out. Since you do not know when you are going to die, you must practice diligently now."

And as a conclusion to each talk he would chant one more poem before descending from his seat. The assembly would finish by chanting the four great vows:

Sentient beings are innumerable, we vow to save them all.
Hindrances are inexhaustible, we vow to overcome them all.
Dharmas are limitless, we vow to learn them all.
The Buddha Way is unsurpassable, we vow to achieve it.

When the lecture was over, the foreign monks and nuns would follow Master Kusan up to his room. I would translate what he had said, and then he would answer questions:

Q: How can one distinguish a wrong view from a right view?
A: A wrong view would be to think of doing something with the idea that it will be beneficial to you. A wrong view would be to think only of amassing intellectual knowledge, or to think that you know a great deal, or to wonder whether you are practicing well or not. You are only meant to investigate the *hwadu* and awaken to the One Mind. You should only think of continuously

practicing the *hwadu* with great energy and vivid doubt. This is the right view.

Q: You have said that while contemplating the *hwadu* one should have no thoughts of any future result, such as enlightenment. Should one likewise discard all beliefs, the belief that all sentient beings are buddhas, for example, or the belief that one has the buddha-nature?

A: Yes, such thoughts should also be discarded. You must let go of everything and only keep "What is this?" Even if the Buddhas and Patriarchs appear before you, they are not what you are seeking. Endeavor to realize that one thing which you do not know. Good, bad, right, wrong: discard them all!

Q: Does the idea of "mind" create a hindrance toward realizing enlightenment?

A: Yes, to call it "mind" is a hindrance, because "mind" is just a name. As though you were a pure sheet of white paper, you should inquire into that which you do not know. Even the slightest thought is an obstacle.

Q: But how can one think "What is this?" without any thought at all?

A: Although you have to begin by thinking, after several hours of practice, when you penetrate deeply into the *hwadu,* all thinking will disappear. At that point the "not-knowing" that clearly appears is what is called the "mass of doubt." Thus it is said:

If there is thought, one cannot realize one's practice.
And if there is no thought, one cannot realize it either.

So, if you hold your *hwadu* and just repeat the question, you are still caught in delusive thinking. But if you continue for many more hours until you penetrate deeply, then delusive thinking will be severed and you will enter one-pointedly.

Q: What is there other than form and emptiness?

A: Does emptiness have a form?

Q: Emptiness and form are not different.

A: So why did you ask that silly question? To think that there is emptiness is a delusive thought; to think that there is form is also a delusive thought. And to think that there is something other than emptiness and form is likewise a delusive thought. They are all delusive thoughts.

Q: In a lecture you once said, "In the middle of a dream, you cannot see the Great Way." What did you mean?

A: I meant that you cannot attain the Great Way by means of material things. Although in China Emperor Wu built many temples and reliquaries, he was unable to awaken to the mind by means of these things. It was the same when I struck my staff upon the platform. You must awaken to the Way in the midst of this sound, but you will never do so by grasping at the form itself.

Q: So "dream" refers to material things?

A: Yes. All material things are like dreams. In them you cannot realize the truth.

Q: How in one's practice can one combine great doubt with great quiescence?

A: When you first give rise to the doubt, it seems as though you are actually "doing" something. But if you penetrate deeply, all sense of "doing" will vanish, and the great doubt alone will remain; this in itself is great quiescence.

Q: Is the doubt something we create, or is it something that has always been present and that we come into contact with through practice?

A: The mass of doubt coalesces through an accumulation of not knowing, which is the result of a consistent and determined practice of meditation. Yes, the doubt is something we create through our own efforts.

Q: But in a sense is it not always there, but we are simply unaware of it?

A: Only if you give rise to doubt and questioning will it be there. Without any such questioning, it will never occur. For this reason, awakening is something which comes about through one's own efforts. Although the mind is fundamentally present, you will never awaken to it without applying yourself. Therefore, the Buddha engaged in ascetic practices for six years and Bodhidharma gazed at a wall for nine. This is the kind of hard practice one must do.

Q: Should one always maintain an attitude of self-reproach?

A: An attitude of self-reproach should arise upon reflecting that because it has been stated that the mind of a buddha and the mind of a sentient being are the same, then why have I been unable to awaken? If you think in this way, self-reproach will arise. Although this attitude is necessary prior to one's awakening, after one has awakened it is no longer needed.

Q: Once while I was feeling lazy, I tried to cultivate self-reproach in order to become more diligent. But as the self-reproach arose, the doubt began to weaken. What should be done about this?

A: If a genuine attitude of self-reproach appears, then this should actually strengthen the doubt. There is no reason for it to weaken the doubt. So what is this attitude of self-reproach? You should only reproach yourself for not having realized the mind. It is because you reproached yourself about something else that the doubt weakened. Only be concerned that you have not yet awakened to the mind. Why is it that you do not yet know what it is? You must understand it. It is not good reproaching yourself about anything else.

Q: So it seems that if self-reproach were developed along with questioning, then the two should coalesce.

A: Yes, this is so.

Q: Should one locate the *hwadu* at a particular point in the body?

A: Concentrating your questioning in one particular place may cause you to cling to that place; this is not very good. After practicing for a while, you might experience a constricted feeling in the chest. This could be the result of your not-knowing and the doubt and questioning produced from that. But if you just continue uninterruptedly, you will pass a critical moment, after which the constricted feeling will dissolve and your practice will become much easier.

Q: So you would not advise us to concentrate on the *tanjon* [i.e., an energy point three fingers below the navel, described in Taoist yoga]?

A: When first practicing meditation you may place your concentration here and focus upon the *hwadu* there. You may also do this if you are worried about contracting *sanggi* [when the energy goes to the head and causes a headache]. This too, however, may become a kind of clinging. When you enter very deeply into the practice, the body and the entire universe will be forgotten and one thought alone will vividly appear. Then the practice will be progressing. So always try to investigate with the mind alone. If you continue exerting yourself in such a way, the body and all its hindrances will slowly dissolve, and a clear, spiritual strength will be generated.

Q: It seems that you advocate living simply in the mountains. But what about going into the world to help others?

A: Ah, this! If you diligently practice and awaken, then you should leave the mountains and guide others. But even if you live in the city and want to guide others, without wisdom you cannot guide anyone.

Q: Does the stone tiger stand for someone who is practicing or for one who is awakened?

A (laughing): The stone tiger roars only after one has awakened.

Q: Is the stone tiger mute before awakening, or does it appear for the first time upon awakening?

A: I told you: you must awaken. Upon awakening, a wooden man will sing and a stone lady will dance. (Laughing.) It is like that.

Sometimes he would catch us out as we drank tea, often the green tea we had all collected in the mountains and roasted in the monastery kitchen. After the first sip he would ask, "Does it taste good?" We would answer "Oh yes, it's very good." Then he would say, "What is it that tastes the tea?" Everyone would remain silent.

For four years I continued my meditation practice while helping with translation and being of service in various ways. It was a challenge to keep to a rigorous schedule as well as to be on call at all times and sometimes have to spend two days transcribing the tape of a lecture. At times I would be with other Western nuns, at other times I would spend the season by myself. When living with other people, friction generally arose at some point or another but because meditation was our common ground, conflicts were usually resolved harmoniously through the wisdom, compassion, and awareness that practice created. To be on my own made me realize that conflicts did not arise outside of myself but from my own attachment and ignorance. Even when no one else was around I still managed to get upset or irritated.

Death of a Zen Master

IN JUNE 1983 Master Kusan's health began to deteriorate. His eyes and his ears began to trouble him, which affected his balance when he was walking. To remedy this condition, he decided to exercise by working in the fields. As the nuns' compound was on the way to the fields, he would often stop by and ask me to join him. I was very happy for these chances to spend time with him informally. In the fields we would pick stones from the earth or cut the blackened diseased heads of the barley. He would sometimes call out to me, "What did Chao-chou mean by 'the cypress in the courtyard'?" I would tell him I did not know. If I had understood, I would have been able to answer spontaneously. He would stress that I should awaken to the meaning of this *koan* by practicing diligently. Then we would rest by the side of the field and he would tell me Zen stories.

During the following free season, his condition deteriorated. I learned from his senior disciples that on his previous birthday he had predicted that he was going to die in June. Although this date passed, he became much weaker and started to meditate day and night in order to be fully ready when the time came. He also composed his death poem.

> The autumn leaves covering the mountain are redder than flowers
> in spring.
> Everything in the universe fully reveals the great power.
> Life is void and death is also void.
> Absorbed in the Buddha's ocean-seal *samadhi*, I depart with a smile.

occasion I went for a walk with him and another monk. We
and sat on a tree trunk. He said, "No matter how much you have
ced, you are never sure how you are going to be at the moment of
ch. You must practice diligently all the time to be as well prepared as
you can be." I was touched by these words; they showed me that he did not
take his achievements for granted. It was very humbling.

Shortly afterward he had a stroke that left him paralyzed on one side.
But even then he would ask to be seated in the cross-legged position and
would spend the day meditating and turning the large beads of his rosary.
When asked why he turned beads, sometimes he said, "I am turning the
wheel of the dharma." At other times he would say that it was just an exercise for his fingers.

Finally, late one night, the main bell was rung. We all knew what it
meant. I started to cry. After a moment or two, I put on my formal robes
and made my way to his room. One by one we all bowed three times before his body, as was the tradition. He had died in the sitting position surrounded by his closest disciples. Later his body was placed in an upright
coffin and put in another larger room, where the monks from the Zen hall
kept a meditative vigil for three days and nights. Monks, nuns, and
laypeople arrived from all over the country to join in the vigil and assist at
the funeral service and cremation. On the night before the funeral, many
people meditated the whole night long, something Master Kusan would
have approved of.

Laywomen decorated his bier with yellow and white chrysanthe-
mums. Colorful banners were inscribed with poems and sacred words,
the foreign nuns and monks preparing theirs in English, French, Sri
Lankan, Danish, and Chinese.

After the memorial ceremony, the bier was carried through the temple
grounds to symbolize his last journey through the monastery to which he
had devoted twenty years of his life, restoring it to its former spiritual
grandeur. The banners fluttered brightly in the wind, sending their mes-
sages to the four corners of the earth.

The procession made its way to the funeral pyre in a nearby rice field.

The bier was removed and the coffin placed over a pit filled with charcoal and wood. The coffin was covered with kindling and logs, which were then lit by the senior monks, shouting as they did so, "It's getting hot! Get out, get out!" As the pyre burst into flame, we had to move back from the heat. It burned fiercely all afternoon and into the night. Some of us stayed beside it all night, meditating. It was a cold, clear night with a nearly full moon shining over the mountains. As the fire dwindled, we moved closer to be kept warm by Master Kusan's burning body. We were all very sad.

The following afternoon, when the ashes and bones had cooled, the monks started sifting through them with long roughly made twig-chopsticks, searching for anything that might be considered a relic. Some of the bone fragments were rich in color, sparkling blue, deep red, bright yellow, and orange. These were passed around for us all to look at. The other Westerners present and I were rather perplexed by these proceedings. It did lighten the mood, however, and people began to smile and thank Master Kusan for these final gifts.

Later that evening I was faced with one of the strangest sights of my life. In the middle of the master's room on a newspaper lay a pile of his bones—practically all that was left of my dear teacher. In a corner, disciples examined the ashes and the smaller bones on a low table, looking for *sarira*, pearl-like drops either embedded in the bones or found loose among the ashes, which were considered to appear only in the remains of highly realized beings. That year two other elder monks had died, but in neither case had any *sarira* been found. In another corner of the room, the abbot tested potential relics by trying to crush anything that was passed to him with a pair of pliers. If it broke, that was a sure sign that it was not a *sarira*. After two days' searching, fifty-three *sarira*s were found and the search was called off. One of the monks was still nonchalantly reading the newspaper on which the bones had been laid.

The following morning all the remaining ashes from the fire pit were scooped away. The bones were crushed between tiles and put with the ashes into a celadon vase. Then all the disciples took the vase to Master Kusan's favorite spot high in the mountains, the site of a hermitage he had once built. The day was crisp and bright, and the river was frozen. Fields of pampas grass swayed in the wind, and the sea shimmered between the mountains tops. Each of us took a handful of the powder and scattered it over the hill, reciting the *Heart Sutra* as we did so. As we made our way back in the dark, our hearts also darkened as we thought of our departed teacher. I recollected the truths of impermanence and the preciousness of this human life.

The following day we were called to his room by his senior disciples, and each of us was given an item from the master's possessions. I was given his waistcoat, which I had mended on several occasions. In this way, all material things associated with him were dispersed. The monastery felt empty without him. It was as though the light had gone out. I realized how much we had taken his presence for granted without recognizing his importance for the spiritual life of the temple. We had become so used to just having him around. But although his death created a profound absence, I slowly discovered that he had not really departed. He was still in my heart. Even now I can hear him telling me to raise the *hwadu* or to take care of my precepts. And I can hear him laughing.

Seeking the Way

Son'gyong Sunim

Son'gyong Sunim.
Photograph by Stephen Batchelor.

⫷ My Autobiography

I WAS BORN on the second of May 1903 in a little village near the city of Ch'ongju. We were peasants, living on a farm and very poor. When I was nine my mother died. I had a brother and a sister older than myself and a younger sister of five. Our father grieved terribly over our mother's death and failed to take good care of us. Life became very difficult, and finally it was so bad that I decided to kill myself. But as soon as I made that decision, I heard a voice from the sky say, "Your affinity with the Buddha is great. Why end your life?" I understood these words to mean that I should become a nun.

So at the age of eighteen, I made my way to a nunnery called Yongunam near the monastery of Magoksa. At first I was refused admission because I was so small. Then an elderly nun, Inu Sunim, said that although I was small, otherwise I looked all right. Thus I was accepted.

The following year the nuns shaved my head, and I received ordination. My preceptress was called Myongdok Sunim. She traveled a great deal from nunnery to nunnery in order to further her meditation practice. Her own preceptress happened to be Inu Sunim, who thus became my elder. She agreed to take charge of me, and for many years I served as her attendant.

Apart from performing the daily services, however, I did not learn anything, nor did I practice meditation, because there was no one there to teach me. My elder was a little worried about this lack, but she contended that because I was so small I could not be sent anywhere else. At that time, all Buddhist books were written in Chinese characters, but I had not yet learned how to read. In those days, women were rarely sent to school. It was thought that a woman who could read and write would be ill-fated in her marriage, for whenever problems arose at her husband's home, she would be able to write back to her own family and complain. I think it was a great fault of the Korean people in the past not to teach women. Now it is different; all young girls go to school, even up to high school. I am glad for them. Nevertheless, although I could not read, I was still expected to learn the chants by heart. So I taught myself the characters of the chants one by one.

My life was hard. I had to wash clothes, prepare food, chop wood, and make fires. Sometimes I even had to go and cut wood in the forest and carry it on a frame on my back. I was very dismayed at having to do this kind of work, because in the villages this was normally the work of the men. Once I remember thinking that life in the nunnery was even worse than life in the village, and I threw down the carrying-frame in disgust. Then I sat down and cried. Because I had damaged the frame slightly, my elder asked me what had happened. I told her, "I am done with that kind of work! I am too small! I am a nun. Why should I do it?" After that, she never asked me to do such things again.

I liked my preceptress very much but rarely saw her. She was from an upper-class family that supported both Magoksa and Yongunam. Being from such a background, she had had some education and knew Chinese characters quite well. After ordination she had studied in a nunnery with a Sutra hall, then gone on to meditate in the Zen halls. She died twenty years ago at the age of seventy-two. There was no doubt that she was a very good nun, as was my elder.

My preceptress was always kind to me and was concerned at my attending the elder instead of her. Every time she came, she told me how worried she was that the elder neither taught me the sutras nor instructed me in meditation. I was so happy when she said such things and wished I could have gone off to practice meditation with her. Some of the nuns even suggested that she take me on her travels. But she was reluctant to leave the elder without an attendant. Nevertheless, she asked me to do what I thought was right. So I stayed.

The elder once tried to teach me to weave. But I couldn't even weave a single piece of cloth properly. My preceptress, on the other hand, was a very gifted weaver and did it all for me. It's not that my elder had any bad intentions. For her, just being a good attendant was enough to fulfill the role of a nun.

I stayed at Yongunam until I was thirty-three. At that time the Japanese were occupying the whole country and were causing many difficulties for the Buddhist community. As a result, the Buddhist Order suggested that in order to consolidate the teachings, the great Zen monks of the time should become abbots of the main temples. As part of this policy, Master Man'gong, the Zen master of Chonghyesa, near Sudoksa, was appointed abbot of Magoksa for three years. In fact, he only stayed for eighteen months; the administrative work was too troublesome for him.

On his very first visit, he encouraged the monks to build a Zen hall. He spoke to them abruptly: "Since you are monks, how is it that you idle away your lives without practicing meditation?" I was thirty-two when I heard that talk and had never heard anything like it before. It was extraordinary and inspired me with great determination to practice. Afterward I pondered quietly and realized that the role of monks and nuns was very different from what I had been led to believe.

Master Man'gong's talks would always accord with his audience. To practitioners, he would talk about meditation; to students of the sutras, he would talk about the *Heart Sutra,* urging them not only to understand its literal meaning but also to awaken to its deeper meaning through practice. I realized that I wanted to find a nunnery near his usual place of residence, Chonghyesa, a hundred kilometers northwest of Magoksa.

On learning of my wishes, my elder refused to let me go. I explained that I wanted to learn more about the true role of a nun. But she countered by saying that to go would not be in accordance with that role. She also questioned my ability to understand dharma talks because I had never heard any before. And she added that one should just live as one lives. There was nothing more to it than that. She even tried to prevent me from leaving by offering me a special position in the nunnery. But it was to no avail. Nothing could deter me. I begged her for four whole days. Finally she gave in and told me I could go for a visit. Without giving me money or quilts, she helped me pack, telling me to have a look and come back soon (previously a nun needed to supply her own quilt; it is not so anymore).

PRACTICING IN THE ZEN HALL

The monastery of Chonghyesa was like another world. When I saw the meditation hall, I felt that the Buddha himself lived there. I wanted to stay at a nearby nuns' Zen hall, Kyongsongam, but had no money for my food. In those days (1936), a nun or a monk had to provide one *mal* (18 liters) of rice per month, which amounted to three *mal* per meditation season. In Kyonsongam this system of payment stopped shortly after I arrived. The meditation monks and nuns rarely had any money, and Master Man'gong thought it was unfair to refuse them on the grounds that they could not provide the three *mal* of rice. He therefore asked some laypeople to help provide enough money to pay at least for the food of the meditators. Thus both in Kyonsongam and Chonghyesa the payment of three *mal* of rice was abolished. Many other temples followed suit. Only temples that had no revenue from large rice fields or that had few supporters were obliged to continue with this system for some time to come.

Because I had no rice or money, they offered me the job of preparing the side dishes in the kitchen for a year. I accepted this job, and in return I was permitted to practice in the Zen hall with the other nuns. During that time, I heard dharma talks by Man'gong Sunim and also by Pophui Sunim, an elderly nun who was the senior advisor at Kyonsongam.

Pophui Sunim was a great Zen nun who had received dharma transmission from Master Man'gong. She had entered the order in infancy and had studied the sutras and Zen records until the age of twenty-five. Thereafter she had practiced meditation under Master Man'gong until her mind-eye opened completely. He gave her the special dharma

name of Myori Pophui (Subtle Principle Dharma Joy) and wrote her this
transmission poem:

> Subtle Principle Bhiksuni Pophui,
> The nirvana of manifold forms
> Is the face of Sakyamuni Buddha;
> The complete disappearance of nirvana
> Is the face of the Patriarch
> Sakyamuni passed away two thousand five hundred years ago,
> But the subtle principle of true light shines always.

Once, Master Man'gong talked of the *koan* "Peach flower blossoms
scatter in the snow." He asked the assembly, "Where are the scattered blossoms of the peach flower?" Pophui Sunim responded, "When the snow
melts, only a lump of earth remains." Master Man'gong said, "Pophui
Sunim has got 'the piece of paper' [i.e., she understands]."

Pophui Sunim traveled to many places to practice, but at the age of
seventy she returned to Sudoksa and became the Zen advisor of Kyongsongam. She was especially kind to me and taught me many profound
things. It pleased her that a young nun had come to practice the way of the
Buddha.

At the end of the year my elder appeared in Kyonsongam, insisting
that she could not live without me, that I alone was capable of serving her
properly. She said that if I did not return with her, she would come and
live with me at Kyongsongam. I refused to return to that kind of existence
because Man'gong Sunim clearly did not approve of it as a way of life for
monks and nuns. He used to say that to live like that would send us to hell
after death. So I entreated her to spend a meditation season there with me,
and she did.

Strangely enough, the communal life of the Zen hall appealed to her.
She commented on how very practical and economical it was to live all together in this way. And since she meditated in the Zen hall and ate formally with the assembly, it was no longer necessary for me to be her

attendant. All I had to do was help her wash her clothes and do some small chores. Sitting in meditation was new to her, but she developed real faith, and great determination arose within her. She continued meditating for two more years in Kyongsongam, after which she returned to Yongunam with another of her disciples as her attendant.

The following year, at the end of the summer period of meditation, my preceptress showed up. She had heard that my elder and I were both practicing in the Zen hall, which had pleased her greatly. My elder then said that my preceptress should teach me and guide my practice and that now I should be her attendant. My elder was very nice to me then and gave me a very good set of clothes.

At that time my preceptress was living in the Zen hall of Yunp'ilam, a nunnery near Mungyong, in the northeastern part of South Korea. She asked me if I wanted to join her there. I accepted, overjoyed at the prospect of spending more time with her. Before leaving, however, I decided I should learn more about the *hwadu* from Master Man'gong. I had never really had the opportunity to ask him questions because I had always been so busy in the kitchen. Although I had listened to his dharma lectures and had tried to put into practice what he advised, I had usually given up after a short while. As yet I had not seriously taken up a *hwadu*. Master Man'gong usually taught the *hwadu*s "The thousand things return to the one, where does the one return?"; "No!"; or "What is this?" I realized that if I really wanted to meditate, I had to have my own *hwadu*.

So one day I visited Master Man'gong in his room. He was sitting there alone. I bowed three times and told him, "I would like to have a *hwadu*. Please teach me one." Although he had seen me enter, he had still not looked up. He just sat there with his eyes closed. I felt very nervous and wondered if he was behaving in this way because he thought that I, being so small, could not practice. I became sad and began to think of all my shortcomings. Then, after about thirty minutes of silence, I decided to leave. At that very moment, he suddenly opened his eyes wide and shouted, "Since you are incapable of knowing where is the head or the tail, what kind of *hwadu* are you talking about?" I was so surprised by this out-burst that my chest felt heavy, and my heart pounded as if I had been struck by a ball. I did not know what to do. I felt so distressed to have been given a scolding instead of a *hwadu* that I scurried out the back door without asking him anything more.

Shortly afterward, I left with my preceptress. I was very glad to go with her, but it felt as though there was a coagulated mass in my chest brought about by the shock of my encounter with Master Man'gong. I was still overwhelmed by distress and worry about not having a *hwadu*.

We traveled to Yunp'ilam by train. It was the first time that I had ever ridden a train. Yunp'ilam was beautiful; I took an immediate liking to it. The first thing we did when we arrived was to bow to everyone; then we settled in. The meditation season was only five days away.

Not long after we arrived, Ch'ongam Sunim, a disciple of Master Man'gong, visited the nunnery from Taesongam, the main monastery nearby, where he held the post of Zen advisor. Although I was worthless, he seemed to like me. (I learned later that he had inquired about where my preceptress's nice new disciple had come from and had questioned my teacher about me.) I told him that I had been the attendant of my elder for a long time but had been unable to learn anything. Then I asked him if he would teach me a little about a *hwadu* so that I could practice meditation properly. He exclaimed, "If you did not learn a *hwadu* from Master Man'gong, from whom will you ever learn?" This distressed me even more, and I pondered on the fact that for a second time a great monk was rebuking me. Once more I was overwhelmed with anxiety and shame.

A few days later, the meditation season began. The entire assembly of nuns held a meeting to decide on the schedule for the forthcoming period and also to appoint the various duties. We decided to begin with a thirty-day period of strenuous meditation practice. Thirty nuns had gathered in the Zen hall, all diligent meditators. But I could not think of practicing se-riously anymore; I just felt great distress and shame at the thought that everyone was probably wondering what on earth I was doing during the meditation periods. I had to make tea in the mornings. For the rest of the time I sat in meditation—sometimes experiencing distressing thoughts, sometimes doubts like "why can't I practice like the others?" and "why do the monks always rebuke me and not give me a *hwadu*?"

For the next twenty-one days, these thoughts of self-reproach did not abate. I lost the need to sleep and spoke to no one. Then I found myself in a state of vivid clarity. At eleven-thirty the other nuns would go to sleep in the meditation hall in their respective places, but I would go to the side room and meditate all night. Slowly, a very vivid and tranquil state of mind arose. All distracted thoughts dissolved away and only clarity and quiescence remained. Occasionally the question "What is this?" would arise. All trace of distress disappeared, leaving the mind clear and pure. My thoughts were overturned and the self-reproach I had been experiencing diminished. Suddenly a single thought pierced right through me, all the way up to the top of my head. The thought was so powerful that a voice came out of me, which said, "Since originally there is no head or tail, where could either of them be?"

Shortly after that, Ch'ongam Sunim came to Yunp'ilam. I told him that the self-reproach had pierced through me to the point where I felt I could toss the great masters over my shoulder. He explained that this was the great doubt on the point of bursting. It still had to grow more before it burst, but once it had, then the practice would progress easily.

The following day he pinned up a notice on the wall of the Zen hall, which read, "Riding the bottomless iron boat, there is no hindrance to crossing the land." When I read this, it suddenly occurred to me that in the midst of mind there are no hindrances. Only the doubt remained, and even that would disappear! The next time we met I told him how I understood the bottomless iron boat to be the mind. I added that because, fundamentally, the mind has no hindrances, it has no difficulties in crossing the land.

He replied that the doubt had now burst and my practice was going well. It seemed that this was the first time he had come across a nun whose doubt had burst so greatly, and it prompted him to return to Chonghyesa to practice with even greater vigor under Master Man'gong. Apparently he was afraid of being surpassed in his practice by a nun.

He must have spoken about me in Chonghyesa and Kyonsongam because at the beginning of the free season, a dharma friend, Pon'gong Sunim, appeared in great haste, saying she was feeling very guilty. Up until now she had thought me to be fit only for the kitchen because of my ugliness and stupidity. Now she had realized these to be misguided thoughts for which she would surely receive karmic retribution. She went on to say that she had not known that when it came down to meditation practice things were different, and she marveled at how I had surpassed her. All this time she had been sitting but never with great courage. After hearing about my experiences, she made bows all night and suggested that from now on we should practice together.

I now had no distracted thoughts at all. My mind was absolutely clear and quiet, and great faith was arising. I was pleased with the faith, which poured out of me, and could think of nothing except practicing meditation.

At that time in Yunp'ilam, there were many nuns who practiced with great determination and who wasted no time on other tasks. Only the kitchen supervisor and the rice cook worked a full day. The kitchen supervisor always said she was glad to take care of her duty while the other nuns were meditating; "each to her own task" was her motto. However, the rice cook suddenly fell ill one day. Feeling ashamed of my idleness, I took this as an opportunity to be of service and decided to take her place, while continuing with the meditation practice. So I would wash and cook the rice as swiftly and efficiently as I could, then go to my place in the meditation hall, endeavoring never to waste a moment.

I was so happy at that time that I could not even sleep, such was my sense of urgency. I was practicing the *hwadu* "All things return to the one, where does the one return?" This *hwadu* had presented itself after the doubt had burst. Now it was there even while I was working and eating.

After a while I became weak and unable to take much food. Only my faith sustained me as I worked. Once I dozed off while cooking rice, and a child appeared before me. He said, "When it is time to practice, you must do so. Do you really think you can practice at any time and progress at any time? Why did you decide to become the rice cook in the middle of your practice? Look at yourself dozing away!" I reflected on this message and thought that this child must have been the youthful form of the Bodhisattva Manjusri. I realized that the practice was of utmost importance and told the other nuns that I could not be the rice cook any longer, especially as the meditation season was almost upon us.

During that summer's meditation season, an event from one of my past lives suddenly appeared. I saw that in a past life I had been an intelligent and handsome monk. I also saw a very pretty girl who had been born from the heavenly realm and had become a nun. I caused this nun to break her precepts. I then died at the age of fifty and was reborn small and ugly but with a pure mind. After the beautiful nun died, she was reborn as the nun who became my elder. While I was with my elder I had often wondered why, regardless of my behavior, she had sometimes liked me and sometimes not. After this vision I understood it was because I had made her break her precepts in a previous life. I did not know whether to take this vision seriously or not, yet felt thoroughly happy about it. I walked up and down outside for two hours, laughing like a madwoman, mistakenly believing the vision to be a sign that the practice was progressing.

For two years my preceptress served as the leader of the meditation hall in Yunp'ilam. At no time did she ask me to attend her, as she thought I had already amply fulfilled my duties as the attendant of my elder. In the Zen hall she simply looked upon me as one of the meditators and never expected me to do special things for her. She was pleased that I had faith in the practice and meditated with diligence. She said that my experience of the doubt bursting would give a good and strong base to my practice. After she left Yunp'ilam, she traveled around the country visiting other meditation halls, where we used to meet whenever possible. At the end of the Korean War, she built a little temple in P'yongt'aek, a town near Seoul, where old and sick nuns from her dharma family could stay. She passed away in the mid-1960s at the age of seventy-one.

SEEKING THE WAY

After nearly four years I left Yunp'ilam. I believe now that had I stayed for a further year I could have completed the task. However, I let myself be overly influenced by a dharma friend for the sole reason that I thought I had to have a dharma friend. This friend was Pon'gong Sunim, who suggested we go to Mount Odae at the beginning of the free season. I agreed enthusiastically, thinking it would be a good place to practice and a good place to complete the task. Before leaving, we performed a special session of chanting. For seven days we observed silence, chanted, and remained standing throughout the day. At the end of it, a young boy appeared before me as if in a dream. Pon'gong Sunim did not see him. I asked him where he had come from and why. He said he had come from Mount Odae, and that the great Zen master Hanam had told him to escort us there. I asked the boy whether he had walked all the way here. He replied that he had not had to walk because he could fly. This apparition was certainly a sign to strengthen our resolve.

So we left. On the way we took the opportunity to visit the Diamond Mountains. It was the first time I had seen such sights. At Podok Cave we performed another seven-day chanting session, then at Naksansa yet another, lasting fourteen days. Toward the end of this chanting session the Bodhisattva Avalokitesvara, whose portrait was above the altar, appeared before me and said, "If you are really intent on practice, why are you wandering idly about? Go quickly to meet the great Zen master! Have a dharma exchange with him and practice hard!" I had never before had any dharma exchanges. At Yunp'ilam there was nobody with whom to have them. In any case, I had always thought it enough just to practice diligently. The bodhisattva appeared to me again and said, "People who are practicing do not walk around for hours on end. Where did all the great teachers and bodhisattvas ever wander? All the buddhas and bodhisattvas are inside us. Why are you exerting yourself in this way? It is all in vain. Stop now. Go to the master and ask him about practice!"

So we carried on in the direction of Master Hanam's monastery. On penetrating the mountainous region around Mount Odae, we came to a small temple. It was getting dark, so we decided to stay the night. The three monks who occupied the temple were very surprised to see us; they were not used to encountering nuns who traveled for the sake of furthering their practice. As it was a very small place, they partitioned off half the main room with a screen and insisted we sleep on the warmest part of the floor. It was the tenth month; snow was falling heavily and we were still forty *li* from Master Hanam's monastery. The monks suggested we traveled via the Sinsollyong Pass, a route they thought would still be quite mild. After eating the rice they offered us, we left early. When we were midway up a mountain, suddenly a young man appeared and wanted to know where we were heading. Having told him, he advised us to sleep that night in a nearby village because we were still far from our destination.

The following morning we set off again. It was a beautiful clear day but at one stage we could not find the right path because of the snow. Only a few days remained before the meditation season was to begin, and yet here we were, unable to either advance or retreat—it was most distressing. Then we heard someone shouting, "What are you doing there? If you make a mistake now you may lose your way and freeze to death!" We begged him to point out the way to us. He told us to go by the middle path. We could only just make it out. Curiously, he seemed to be the same person we had met the day before.

Sliding a lot, we managed to make the ascent without hurting ourselves. At the top, some Japanese were selling hot tea. We rested there and Pon'gong Sunim expressed her anger. "To travel with a crooked-nosed midget like you indeed makes the going tough! If only I had been by myself I would have taken a vehicle and would not have had to put up with all these hardships." To which I replied, "I am so grateful to you. If you had not been my dharma friend, never would I have known where the Diamond Mountains or Mount Odae were. Thank you so much for taking me to such beautiful places." She laughed heartily and excused herself for having spoken with anger; it was just that it had been very difficult, and she had become annoyed. She promised not to speak like that again.

Eventually, dripping wet, we reached Sangwonsa. When we met Master Hanam, he was horrified to learn of the route we had taken in order to get there. Apparently even people who knew their way around those parts had frozen to death on the path we had taken. We told him how a young man had helped us. He commented that sometimes the Bodhisattva Manjusri revealed himself to the faithful when they were lost in the mountains.

After our interview, we discovered that five other nuns had arrived from Yunp'ilam. This made us very happy because there were eighty monks in residence. After breakfast the following day, the seven of us went to bow formally to enter the assembly. The monks were very surprised to see seven nuns—the previous evening there had only been two—and they refused to accept us. The leader of the Zen hall told us not to bow and asked us to leave. We were at a loss as to what to do next. Pon'gong Sunim asked if we could spend the season working in the kitchen, but the monks told us that also was not possible. But then Master Hanam very kindly told us about Chijangam, a hermitage thirty *li* away built as a Zen hall for nuns by a layperson, where we might be accepted for the meditation season. We were told that if it worked out, we could return in two days for the inaugural lecture of the retreat. I was overjoyed at the prospect, and we all went there. The abbess of Chijangam turned out to be a dharma friend. She lived there with only one disciple and was glad to have us.

On the first day of the meditation season, we had baths, shaved our heads, and walked back to the monastery to listen to Master Hanam's lecture. He was very pleased to see us. This first lecture was about the *Platform Sutra,* and I felt I could understand everything he said. Master Hanam was most compassionate, almost motherlike in the way he endeavored to make us understand and investigate. He knew that I had come from Master Man'gong's place and was working on a *hwadu,* but I did not ask him about it when I first saw him. In fact, I never really engaged in dharma exchanges with him; my purpose in being there was purely to study under his direction, practice as hard as I could to awaken, and then return to see Master Man'gong.

We were pleased with the way things had turned out. The main temple near Chijangam was a place called Wolchongsa. The abbot was so glad to have nuns from the province of Ch'ungnam meditating in the little hermitage under his jurisdiction that he sent us food, wood, and other supplies to help us out. Pon'gong Sunim was overjoyed at our situation and suggested that we stay for a while.

The following year, Wolchongsa gave us several large fields in which to cultivate potatoes and corn. So in the spring we planted crops. However, perhaps because of all the traveling, I became utterly exhausted. The food was so bad that my appetite left me; I lost a lot of weight and became depressed. Moreover, I was asked to be kitchen supervisor, which I initially refused on the grounds of ill health, but since there was no one else to do it, reluctantly I took it on.

Not long afterward, an old nun asked if one of us would look after her small temple in the province of Kangnung. As it was the free season, I volunteered to go. But the food there was also very poor. In those days, nuns who practiced meditation were not taken very seriously. Added to that, the old nun had locked the warehouse where the rice was stored before she went away, leaving me with only a meager diet of potatoes and corn. I was not used to such food; until then I had always had at least some rice to eat. Soon I began to feel dizzy. Then my whole body turned yellow with jaundice.

Some visiting nuns suggested I return to Chijangam, but I would rather have died than to fail in my duty. Besides, the old nun was to return shortly. By then I had turned really yellow and, although I had no pain, I had no energy whatsoever. I could only eat the *moku* stalks, which a younger dharma sister who had come to stay prepared and entreated me to eat. At least they had a sweet taste, which I enjoyed.

Then I had a dream. A young boy of fourteen or so appeared before me with a shining bronze bowl filled with steaming sticky rice. He gave it to me and said that the inflammation due to malnutrition would be cured and I would recover. I ate it all, and within three days my face regained its color and my hunger disappeared. I felt now that I would live. My young dharma sister thought that because of my sincere practice, a guardian deity had protected me. Shortly after that incident, the old nun came back, and I returned to Chijangam.

Upon my arrival I had another dream. Pon'gong Sunim and I were walking along a path when we met some children digging the ground. When I asked them what they were doing, they said that they were extracting all kinds of medicines, and they gave us each a small piece. As I swallowed mine, I smelled a wonderful fragrance and my mind became peaceful and open. It was very refreshing and gave new strength to my faith. After that, my health and appetite were completely restored.

Once when Pon'gong Sunim went off on some business, she asked me to gather acorns for food. So once a week I picked acorns with five of the local children. Sometimes we would hear noises in the forest. Although I knew the noise was made by a mountain tiger, I would tell the children that it was a pheasant making its nest or flying away, but I would quickly take them back to the temple. Anyway, during Pon'gong Sunim's absence we managed to gather a hundred *mal* and prepare them as jelly. It was a lot of work, but we were diligent and did it quickly. During the Japanese occupation, rice was scarce, and we were often hungry. Acorn jelly was a welcome change from corn and potatoes and felt good for the digestion.

When I was completely well, I had another dream, in which I climbed up to Sangwonsa. Upon passing through the temple gate, I heard the sound of rice being pounded in a water mill. It struck me as strange for there to be a water mill, because the monastery had no water running nearby. Then I heard a voice asking me what water mill I could be thinking of—this was just a normal mill. After that a young boy appeared and asked if I had come to visit the Zen master and wanted to be shown to his room. I told him that I knew where the room was. As I approached I noticed another small room, from which the sun was shining with a bright and warm light. When I opened the door, an old man with frizzy white hair like Master Man'gong's was sitting inside making straw sandals. He had just finished one sandal and was starting on another. I put on the one he had made, and it fitted perfectly. Then I asked, "Oh Zen Master, is it you who are making sandals?"

"Who else?" he replied.

"This one fits my foot perfectly," I said.

"If one fits, all fit!" he said sharply as he glanced across at me. Still wearing the sandal, I stood up. Then he asked me to say something about my time in Yunp'ilam. I told him about some of my experiences, to which he said, "You should know the place in which the Venerable One resides, shouldn't you?" I gave a shout. The old monk laughed. I have no doubts that this old monk was the Bodhisattva Manjusri.

I practiced meditation as much as I could in Chijangam. Nonetheless, I had to take care of a great deal of other things as well, which might have been a mistake at such a time in my practice. Although I continually investigated the *hwadu* "Return to the one," because the doubt had burst once before I had the feeling I knew the answer to the question, which consequently meant that my doubt was not as strong as it should have been. I kept holding the *hwadu* but without great inquiry. I should have asked Master Hanam about this, but all the while I was thinking I would wait and ask Master Man'gong Sunim.

At the end of the meditation season, all the nuns decided to climb up to Sangwonsa to offer good wishes to Master Hanam on his birthday. It was also the right time for picking wild greens, and so on the way we decided to pick a few for the temple. Seventeen of us walked up to a place called Puktae, where the best wild greens grew. Somehow another nun and I strayed from the others and completely lost our way. When we saw the pass of Sinsollyong to one side, we realized just how far we had gone. Being lost this deep in the mountains meant we would certainly become food for the tigers. We threw away the wild greens and ran as quickly as possible along the river. Evening fell, but we just kept running as fast as we could. Finally we saw a house in the distance. We shouted for help. A man called back and told us we were about fifty *li* from Puktae. He advised us to go to Kwangdae, thirty *li* away. So we ran all the way to Kwangdae where we met up with Pon'gong Sunim and the other nuns. They had attended the evening service in Sangwonsa and were returning via Kwangdae in the hope of meeting us there. When Pon'gong Sunim saw us, she screamed that she always got into trouble when she took me anywhere. I apologized profusely, filled with sorrow and shame at having caused so much worry.

Pon'gong Sunim said that she had prepared food for us at Puktae. So we went back there with the intention of visiting Sangwonsa the next day to ask forgiveness. Night had fallen by the time we arrived, and it was very dark. Puktae was just an uninhabited temple, but because we were so full of sorrow at what had happened, we did not feel afraid. My dharma sister went straight to sleep, but I just sat, unable to sleep because of the shame. I felt nothing, no pain and no hunger, just the piercing sense of having made others unhappy. Yet by the middle of the night, my shame had transformed into a state of clarity and quiescence. My mind held no thoughts, just the *hwadu*. Suddenly there was a swishing sound, and the candle blew out. My friend kept snoring. Had I been nervous I would have died at that moment. But I simply stood up, relit the candle, and resumed the sitting. I reflected on a Zen master called Naong, who had lived in this place long ago, and thought of the hardships he must have endured.

The following morning, while my friend prepared rice, I wandered around picking some more greens. Then we went down to Sangwonsa, our packs stuffed with fresh greens. I felt as if I could fly. When we entered Master Hanam's room, he asked if we were the nuns who had been lost the previous day. We told him the whole story. When I mentioned feeling ashamed for our misdeeds, he exclaimed, "Misdeeds! What misdeeds? You had a virtuous, not an evil, intention. Why didn't you come to sleep here?" I told him that I had been unable to sleep and had meditated all night. He congratulated me on my practice and said that we were only able to stay in Puktae because of my good meditation. "That was a spirit who blew out your candle," he said. "It has been up there for three years now. A thief from a village in the valley went up one day and tried to steal the rice from the monk who was practicing there. The monk was killed in the ensuing fight. Because he fought with the thief, the monk became a spirit. This would not have happened if he had died quietly with a virtuous mind. But by fighting, his actions made him no better than the thief. The only way he can be saved now is through our prayers, chanting, and meditation."

Master Hanam told us to rest and have some lunch. We had to decline because the other nuns would probably be worrying about us again by now. He was so pleased with the way we had behaved that he accompanied us back to Kwangtae. When we returned to Chijangam, Pon'gong Sunim took hold of our wrists and said, "Ah! They did not die; they came back alive!" and laughed. She no longer harbored any ill feelings and was, we realized, rather guilty for having subjected us to the hardships of Puktae. Not long after that, she left for another Zen hall at Kugilam, a nunnery near Haeinsa.

TAKING ON MONASTIC DUTIES

It was around this time that I heard the sad news of Master Man'gong's death. I cried a great deal because I had been looking forward to visiting him for a dharma exchange. Master Man'gong had been like a fierce and abrupt father. He would only listen to words of awakening and always tried to help people arouse the true mind. Sometimes he would write to meditators during the second half of the meditation season. He even sent me a letter once at Yunp'ilam, in which he asked me to write and tell him what my questions were. I wrote, "After boiling a rock until it is soft, I will offer it to the good-knowing advisor." He replied that he preferred his rock uncooked.

I was unable to attend either the funeral or the forty-ninth-day death ceremony. However, I was determined to attend the hundredth-day ceremony, which was to occur during the second lunar month. So I traveled to his monastery, Sudoksa, with another nun and took part in the ceremony. Afterward, Pophui Sunim, the Zen advisor for the nuns at the nearby Kyongsongam, advised me not to return to Chijangam. Moreover, the abbess of the nunnery emphasized how important it was for me to spend the coming season with a large assembly to meditate and attend to other duties. I argued that I had to go back to Chijangam because I had not brought a quilt and my backpack was empty. She said that other nuns could bring my things when they came by Kyongsongam. Since she insisted so much, I had no choice but to spend the summer at Kyongsongam.

I was immediately given the job of food supervisor. Even before completing the allotted period for this duty, however, I was asked to serve as kitchen assistant instead. It seems that they really did not want me to go away. I tried to refuse this job on the grounds that I did not know how to handle money, shop in the market, or speak properly. I was told that I would be given help and heard someone say impatiently, "Who do these young people think they are, just wandering about from Zen hall to Zen hall without ever assuming any responsibilities? It won't do!" So I took on the position of kitchen assistant for the next three years and practiced in the Zen hall whenever I had some time off. Once, when I was meditating early one morning, I felt as though I had been struck by a thunderbolt and that a piece of the moon had entered me. My mind was very clear, and my body felt as if it had blown away. I shouted, "I am liberated from birth and death!" Everyone in the Zen hall was startled and no doubt wondered what kind of dream I had been having. So I left the room, chuckling to myself, and walked about quietly outside for a while.

Before the three years were up, I made up my mind to leave and thoroughly cleaned the kitchen in preparation. However, the night before I planned to make my three formal bows of departure in the main hall, Master Man'gong appeared to me in a dream. He asked the celebrant to beat the wooden bell to call the kitchen assistant. For a deceased Zen master to be concerned about a humble kitchen assistant made me think that I must have performed my duty badly. I put on my gown and formal robe, then entered his room to bow. He looked so alive that it did not feel like a dream at all. As I was bowing he said, "I heard that you are quitting your duty."

"Yes, I'm leaving," I replied in a small voice.

He said, "You must finish your full three years, only then will you conclude your task." But I insisted that I had made up my mind and would leave the next day.

And that morning I did indeed make my formal bows to the assembly. Shortly afterward Kobong Sunim, the new Zen master at Chonghyesa, asked for the kitchen assistant to go and see him. I went, and he told me, "You have made a mistake. The community asked me to persuade you to complete the full three years of your responsibilities. If the community approves of something, then it is certain that the Buddha approves of it. I heard about your experiences in Yunp'ilam and am convinced that if you stay the full three years at Kyongsongam, you will finish your task." I replied to the effect that I had had enough and was going.

The following day, I dreamed that I was in an orchard of peach trees. Numerous large peaches were hanging from their branches, and I picked some to offer to the Zen master and the community. Then suddenly all the peaches transformed into thousand-bead rosaries. I picked them up one by one and carried them in my arms.

Later I had another dream that impressed upon me that if I completed the full three years at Kyongsongam, I would complete all the meritorious actions necessary. But if I failed to complete these actions, then I would be unable to give dharma talks; in fact, this turned out to be true. I have never been able to give dharma talks.

So, despite these dreams and the entreaty of Kobong Sunim, I relinquished my post. Pophui Sunim suggested that I rest from my years as kitchen assistant and invited me to accompany her to a nunnery she was to take care of near Seoul. It was not a temple as such, but the country villa of President Syngman Rhee, which had been turned into a Zen hall. The nun who was kitchen assistant there was the niece of the president's secretary.

I accepted gladly Pophui Sunim's invitation. The day before the next meditation season began, we held the usual meeting to decide on the duties of each participant. The assembly wanted me to strike the wooden clapper and thus become the leader of the hall. I tried to refuse on the grounds that I was too old and did not know how to do it. But they insisted: "You should know how to do it. We've all heard of your experiences in Yunp'ilam."

"I'm speechless," I replied.

"If you're speechless, then I'll speak for you," someone retorted. "Just do it!" So I spent the summer being the leader of the Zen hall. We all practiced diligently, and the season went well.

At the beginning of the free season, I told Pophui Sunim I had to visit my elder in Magoksa for a short while. Although I arrived there without even my backpack, owing to the outbreak of the Korean War it was three years before I could leave. The communists had threatened to kill the great monks, so many of them as well as other practitioners sought refuge in Magoksa. It was said that the monastery was protected by the gods. And it was true; we were left completely untouched by the war.

Two Zen halls were established there during that time. The monks established the Ungjokam Zen hall, and I organized a Zen hall for the nuns at Yongunam, the hermitage where I had been ordained, and became its leader. Many nuns came here from Kyonsongam, making a total of about thirty. My relationship with my elder was good now, and she sat with us in the hall, happy that I was practicing well. She never asked me to be her attendant again. After meditating sincerely, without missing any hours of the schedule, she died there at the age of eighty-five in 1954.

After the war, Pon'gong Sunim came to Magoksa and suggested that we go to study together at Tonghwasa, a monastery near the city of Daegu, where Zen Master Hyobong was residing. I spent two years there. I remember him giving a lecture once in which he said, "There is a high platform in the sky. Where should the Buddha stand?" I went and stood in front of him. He laughed and said that I had understood. On another occasion, Master Hyobong received some leaves in an envelope from Master Kyongbong. He asked us the meaning of this. I said, "He had already got it wrong when he picked the leaves." Master Hyobong was very compassionate, always trying to help people investigate and understand. My practice went well while listening to his lectures.

After leaving Tonghwasa, Pon'gong Sunim and I wandered for three years, meditating here and there. We ended up in the city of Namhae, where there is a special temple that Zen nuns and monks use to perform chanting sessions. We stayed in a little hermitage nearby that had been built by a laywoman. We would go to Namhae for seven days of chanting and then come back to the hermitage to practice meditation. I stayed there for three years, but only during the first season did I perform the chanting sessions.

A RESPECTED NUN'S LIFE

Toward the end of the Korean War, I had taken charge of my first disciple. A monk had brought her to the temple and told her to bow to the nun she would like to have as her teacher. She bowed to me. As she was already quite old, I was afraid she would not be able to study the sutras well because of the need to memorize so many texts. So after two years, I sent her to Zen halls where there were good nun teachers, such as Pophui Sunim and Mansong Sunim. She had especially liked Mansong Sunim.

Mansong Sunim was born in 1897 in a poor farmer's family. She was married at a young age but, to her great distress, lost her husband very soon afterward. One day she went to Sangwonsa to hear a dharma talk from Master Hanam. His talk comforted her, and she asked him, "I have heard there is a method for invoking the spirit of the dead. I have no other wishes but to meet my husband one more time." Master Hanam looked at her carefully and said, "You can only meet him if you become a nun. If you want to be free of suffering, take refuge in the Buddha!"

Later she visited Master Man'gong, who taught her to investigate a *hwadu* and said to her, "For someone with a superior root it takes seven days; for someone with a medium root it takes twenty-one days, and for someone with a lower root it takes a hundred days." She set herself the limit of a hundred days and gave herself totally to the practice. As a result she contracted *sanggi*. When he learned of her difficulty, Master Man'gong taught her to place her attention in the *tanjon*. By focusing her meditation and breath in the belly, her *sanggi* was cured.

After the hundred days she redoubled her efforts and continued to investigate her *hwadu* for five years, still as a laywoman, until she received confirmation of her awakening from Master Man'gong. Unfortunately

Master Man'gong's poem of transmission to her has been lost. Shortly afterward, in 1936 at the age of thirty-nine, she became a nun and Master Man'gong gave her the dharma name of Mansong (Manifold Nature). Thereafter she devoted herself totally to the practice of Zen meditation.

She eventually became the leader of the Zen hall in a nunnery near Pusan called Taesongam. Her method of teaching was very simple. One day as the nuns were grinding soya beans to make tofu, she asked them, "What is turning: your hands or the millstone?" The nuns remained silent. She clicked her tongue and left. She emphasized the fact of practicing continuously without differentiating between the beginning and end of the sitting period. In such ways she infused the young nuns with great ardor for meditation.

When she first arrived in Taesongam, it was very poor, and food was scarce. So she went to a special chanting hermitage, Sariam, near the large nunnery of Unmunsa. On the night of the last day of the chanting session, she dreamed that a saint gave her two scoops of rice and told her to take them with her. After that chanting session until the present day, food never lacked in Taesongam.

As she grew older she put all her strength into cherishing and protecting the community, to the point that there was not a single place in the grounds of the nunnery that her hands had not touched. Her nature was frank, stern, and severe, but she could also be kind and concerned. She became a living symbol of a committed practitioner for many Zen nuns.

I had not seen my disciple in a long time, then one day she showed up at the hermitage. She said that I had become thin and that my clothes were very poor. So she encouraged me to come back with her to Taesongam, the nunnery of Mansong Sunim. Although Pon'gong Sunim was annoyed that I should pay heed to my disciple, her suggestion actually corresponded very well with my own wishes. So I decided to go, Pon'gong Sunim promising to join us later.

Mansong Sunim took great care of me and provided me with medicines such that my face became quite full. Once Mansong Sunim and I went to the river bank. She asked, "Is it the river that flows or the wind that blows?" I replied, "It is your mind that flows." She laughed. This is the only time we ever had such a dharma exchange.

Then we went together to Naewonsa to help with a special death ceremony. Mansong Sunim would have liked to take me back with her, but the nuns in Naewonsa wanted me to stay on as their Zen advisor. By becoming a permanent resident, I would be able to take care of the young Zen nuns who came to practice. Until then, it was the custom for nuns only to stay for the meditation seasons, leaving the place rather empty in between. The abbess, Suok Sunim, begged me to consider the nunnery my home and thereby encourage nuns to live there all year round.

Suok Sunim had been a disciple of Pophui Sunim since the age of sixteen. After spending many years studying Buddhist doctrine in both Korea and Japan, she practiced for seven years in Zen halls before arriving at Naewonsa, which had been burned down during the Korean War. She took on the responsibility of rebuilding the nunnery, and it soon became one of the foremost Zen halls for nuns in Korea. At the ground-breaking ceremony to start reconstruction, Master Kyongbong wrote a poem for her:

Building a temple, cultivating the mind,
She is pure like a diamond.
In an ancient place on Mount Ch'onsong
She erects the temple anew.
The brightness of the way, the virtue of her wisdom
Are as deep as the sea;
She will certainly achieve her task,
Leaving her mind at ease.

Suok Sunim was also recognized for her poetry. Here are a couple of her verses:

Quiet mind no different from the mountain—
What pleasure dwells in glory and desire?

Let's whisper sutras, purify our minds,
Indifferent to the judgments of the world.

Look! Look! This one thing does not see!
What is my true form in the midst of this?
No sound nor fragrance, always very tranquil,
I walk alone in windswept moonlight.

I greatly enjoyed staying in Naewonsa and became very enthusiastic. The two masters who visited regularly, Master Hyanggok and Master Kyongbong, inspired me greatly. This was especially helpful because my determination had weakened considerably after the death of Master Man'gong. Working on the *hwadu* "Return to the one," I understood that everything returns to the one, and the one returns to the midst of the mind and finishes there. After listening to Master Hyanggok, however, I adopted the *hwadu* "No!" and have practiced that ever since.

Master Kyongbong once wrote on a piece of paper, "Where do all the sutras come from? Where did the Buddha get them from?" I asked him, "Why, great monk, do you bother with distracted thoughts like that?" He nodded and laughed. Although Master Kyongbong was kind, I did not feel strongly inclined to discuss my practice with him. Perhaps it was because he was so old and frail and would leave immediately after his talks.

Master Hyanggok, on the other hand, was strong and rough, indeed quite frightening. I remember him shouting at us once, " 'You are here in great numbers, but what are you doing? Eating food, taking care of yourselves, sightseeing, just gobbling up the rice of the laity? Why are you playing around all day? Why don't you practice?" Then he gave a talk. Just before the end he shouted, "Ten thousand Manjusris are here. Find the true and original one!" and stormed off to his room. I ran after him in my formal robes, shouting, "The true Manjusri, the buddhas of the three periods, the patriarchs of the lineage, the masters of the present age, they all come out of my nostrils!" He laughed and asked, "Where are your nostrils?" I answered, "Originally there are no nostrils, but as I cannot speak without saying something, I said it in this way." He laughed again and said, "You put much effort into your practice. Make the young nuns practice well and guide them." Shortly after this encounter, he died. He had given this lecture because he knew he did not have long to live.

I had had many such dharma exchanges with Master Hyanggok. After his excellent dharma lectures, he would invite us to ask him questions. He would also question us very sharply. Once I went to his room, but he was not there. When he returned I asked him where he had been. He said he had been to bow in the Buddha hall. I asked, "Is that where the Buddha is, then?" He just laughed. I continued, "If that's where the Buddha is, then I'm going to take the Buddha statue and throw it in the river." He laughed even more and replied, "Long ago I spent many years here. I really wanted to bow to that Buddha again."

On another occasion, at the end of a lecture on liberation, he said, "I'll tell you what: If I undress, will you undress as well?" I replied, "If you undress, that's fine; I'll undress as well. On second thought, I won't, because I fear sentient beings will fall into hell." To this he said, "It's the same for me. Although I could undress in front of you, I fear for the negative karma of others, so I will keep my clothes on." We both laughed.

Once Master Hyanggok tested us about the *koan* "Nan-ch'uan kills a cat." This well-known *koan* is recorded in the *Blue Cliff Record* in this way: "At Nan-ch'uan's place one day, the monks of the eastern and western halls were arguing about a cat. When Master Nan-ch'uan saw this, he held up the cat and said, 'If you can speak, I will not kill it.' No one in the community could say anything. So Nan-ch'uan cut the cat into two pieces. Nan-ch'uan questioned Chao-chou with this story. Chou immediately took off his straw sandals, placed them on his head, and made to leave. Nan-ch'uan said, 'If you had been here, you could have saved the cat.' "

Master Hyanggok asked, "Why was he leaving the room with the sandals on his head?" As I was about to make the sound of a cat, Master Hyanggok said, "Don't make the sound of a cat!" I tapped the floor twice with the palm of my hand. He did the same.

My faith and determination were always strengthened by his talks.

Sometimes I understood easily and sometimes I did not. Once he said, "A Chinese horse eats gruel and a Korean pig's belly bursts. What to do?" I said, "Ouch! Ouch! My belly hurts!" He laughed and went out of the room quickly without a word, which meant that what I said was correct.

Pon'gong Sunim arrived at Naewonsa shortly after my appointment and became the leader of the Zen hall for three seasons. Then she left, and shortly afterward she died. The abbess suggested I take charge of the wooden clapper as there was no one else to do it. I agreed and am still the leader today.

I have been here at Naewonsa for about fifteen years. When I was younger, the practice was so urgent, I barely had the time to eat. If I had worked the full three years that time in Kyongsongam, I'm sure I could have finished the task. When I listen to the dharma talks of great monks, I realize that there are many things I know and just as many that I do not. Master Hyanggok and Master Kyongbong are both dead now. And I have lived far too long. I entered the Zen hall when I was thirty-two and have grown old in it.

[In 1983 Son'gyong Sunim had a fall and hurt herself badly. After a few months she decided to leave Naewonsa, feeling she was too great a burden on the Zen hall. She stayed for two years in a suburb of Pusan in the small nunnery of her first disciple. Later she moved to the town of P'yongt'aek near Seoul to the nunnery built by her preceptress, where she was taken care of by her own disciples. She wrote to me occasionally, encouraging me to practice hard while I was still young and full of energy. I met her again in 1992, but she was very unwell and, although happy to see me, barely recognized me. She died in 1994.—MB]

Naewonsa nunnery.
Photograph by Martine Batchelor.

ᳱ An Interview

[AFTER SON'GYONG SUNIM FINISHED telling me her life story, I was curious to know how she felt about the current situation for nuns practicing in Korea. I arranged to have a short interview with her on this topic.—MB]

Q: Compared to now, was the quality of nuns' meditation practice better in the past?

A: It might have been a little better in the past. Then a lot of nuns raised great courage, and their faith was deeper. These days, however sincere the nuns motivation to meditate, it does not seem to compare.

Q: Why?

A: I don't know. It seems their faith is not as deep as before.

Q: But wasn't it more difficult long ago?

A: Yes, it was. Yet although there were fewer nuns, when they decided to practice, they did so totally. When we practiced in Yunp'ilam, we all sat upright, very determined, with our eyes straight. Nobody would talk. We would all practice fearlessly until late at night. Nowadays, there are few people like that. Nobody sits with bright eyes. They all doze, leave the hall, eat in between sittings, or wash clothes. Everyday they are washing clothes. Indeed there is too much of washing clothes nowadays. However, I must say that now in Naewonsa, since they have started a three-year meditation period, the nuns here are practicing better.

It is true that in our times, there were a lot of hardships that nuns do not have nowadays. The standard of living is better now. Nuns have more freedom. Long ago, it was not like this at all. We could not do as we wanted. Food was very meager. So meager that on Mount Odae, I would feel faint while working.

Q: What level of insight do the nuns achieve nowadays?

A: When I look quietly at the nuns practicing in Naewonsa, there seems to be no one who is able to say something meaningful from deep within themselves. Of course, I do not know how they are really doing inside themselves. They are reading passages in the sutras and seem to have more of an intellectual understanding.

Q: But aren't there many more nuns now?

A: Yes, there are many more now. But they seem to progress more by reasoning about what they have read in the sutras.

Q: How do you think the future will develop?

A: I am afraid that the practice might weaken. The nuns do not think of practice and awakening as much. They prefer to use reasoning. Even if they practice three years continuously, less comes out of it. Long ago, without even practicing for three years, something would happen. Under Pophui Sunim, many people practiced very hard and had some experiences. Once, even the kitchen supervisor had an opening and rushed up to Master Man'gong. There were many nuns who would declare such openings to their teacher. In my time, nuns had great determination; it is when you have great determination that you obtain strength in your practice.

Q: What should one do to practice well?

A: To practice well one should generate great courage and great faith. One should be careful about eating and meditate diligently. To develop faith one needs to study with a good teacher. One must be serious in all one's activities. One should also perform austerities, if the practice is to progress. These days, no one performs austerities. This is unprecedented. When I tell the young nuns to live more austerely, they do not like to listen to such words.

For the *hwadu* to progress well, one should never forget the *hwadu*. Day and night, awake or asleep, one should strive diligently and not let the *hwadu* slip away. When I was young, the thought of practicing was so urgent that I did not even have any spare time to eat.

Korean nuns meditating.
Photograph by Martine Batchelor.

🐟 Poems

THE BOTTOMLESS BOAT

Inside the bottomless boat
This old body follows
The nuns up to Vairocana Hermitage,
Where the mountains piercing the sky
And the brook murmuring below
Are bodies of Vairocana,
Original sources of all Buddhas,
True nature of all Buddhas.

Over the ravine's edge I see
Brilliant stupas of ice and snow,
Jade colored bodies of Manjushri,
His laughter the gurgling waters.
The nuns above are eating,
Peering back for ancient tracks,
Like the assembly on Vulture's Peak
At the time of Sakyamuni.

If they all set sail in the bottomless boat,
It would still be empty.
So huge is it
The universe would not fill it;
So tiny is it

You could fit it in a speck of dust.
No form, no color, no words express it:
The abode of suchness which everyone is.

Descending from the Vairocana Hermitage,
I enter the Zen hall
To hear the Bodhisattva reveal
The unsurpassable Dharma.

THE ORIGINAL MIND OF SENTIENT BEINGS

Empty is the original mind of sentient creatures,
Unsubstantial is their being:
Where could a Buddha be born?
Following the Way they rise to Buddhahood;
Committing a crime they fall into hell,
What futile information!

STONE HORSE EMANATES LIGHT

A cow chewing the hair of a ghost's fart
Crashes through an iron wall and bellows,
The tip of a hair of a stone horse emanates light.

THE CLEAR AUTUMN MOONLIGHT

Clear water flows on white rock,
The autumn moon shines bright,
So clear is the original face.
Who dares say it is or is not?

BUDDHA CANNOT SEE BUDDHA

Buddha cannot see Buddha
Sees Buddha.
I cannot see I
Sees I.
"I saw the nature,
Awakened to the Way."
What rubbish!

A THOUSAND HANDS, A THOUSAND EYES

Thousand-eyed Lokeshvara cannot see,
Thousand-handed Lokeshvara cannot touch.
Climbing Mount Ch'onsong
I clap my hands and burst with laughter.

ON THE AVATAMSAKA PLATEAU ON MOUNT CH'ONSONG

After fierce practice on the eighth day of the last month,
We climb in the bottomless boat, panting and heaving up Mount
    Ch'onsong,
To the Avatamsaka Plateau where Wonhyo preached the Dharma.
Among quiet blue mountains and leisurely clouds,
This happy old nun surveys the eternal mountains and rivers,
The steep hillsides, dark valleys spread out at her feet,
The heavens piercing her eyes.
This thing which has no form is free;
With supernatural power and subtle function
It comes and goes in an instant, unobstructed, not leaving a trace.
So one thought repeats the distant birth of the past.

THIS THING

Coming, going, seeing, hearing: this marvelous thing!

Huge, it covers the sky,
Small, it enters a speck of dust,
Bright, like sun and moon,
Dark, like a lacquer barrel.
Mountains, rivers, great earth:
They are but this thing.
To speak of being or nonbeing
Is the dispute of Shaolin.
Avoid such useless words!

WINTER RETREAT IN NAEWONSA ZEN HALL

Outside the Zen hall of Naewonsa
The snow-covered world
Is the garment of Avalokitesvara
Expounding, like flowing water,
The Dharma inexpressible by the body,
Inaudible to the body,
Invisible to the body,
Inexpressible by, inaudible and invisible to space.
So who is this wonderful person
Who expresses, hears, and sees it?

BIRTH, DEATH, NIRVANA: ALL DREAMS

Morning meditation over I leave the hall
To greet the singing birds,
The luxurious shades of mountain trees,
A thousand perfumed flowers,
A hundred sparkling grasses,
All the body of Vairocana,
Original source of the Buddha,
So vivid and clear.
If all this arises through one body,
Why, then, birth and death,
Confusion and enlightenment?
As the original source
Birth, death, nirvana—all dreams;
Ordinary and sacred—both dreams;
Samsara and liberation—only dreams.

THE PLACE OF THE MIND

Among the ten thousand dharmas
Mind nature is the host
Which cannot be taught through words,
Shown in forms,
Conceived in thought,
Heard by ears,
Or seen by eyes,
Yet always shines numinous and vivid,
Lord of the ten thousand dharmas,
The host of the universe.

GLOSSARY

SELECTED READINGS

⌇ Glossary

Ch.: Chinese; Jap.: Japanese; K.: Korean; Skt.: Sanskrit

Am (K.): Hermitage (e.g., Kyongsongam: Kyongsong Hermitage).

Ananda: The cousin and personal attendant of the Buddha.

Avalokiteshvara (Skt.): A bodhisattva who personifies compassion; widely worshipped in Mahayana Buddhist countries.

Bhiksuni (Skt.): A fully ordained Buddhist nun; also *pikkuni.*

Bodhidharma (ca. 4th–5th century CE): The first Chinese Ch'an patriarch.

Bodhisattva (Skt.): Lit. an "awakening being." A person who aspires to become a Buddha for the benefit of others.

Bodhisattva Precepts: The fifty-eight precepts found in the Brahmajala Sutra (Fan-wan ching [Ch.]; Pommang kyong [K.]) and recited and taken repeatedly by the Korean monastics and laypeople.

Bodhi Tree *(ficus religiosa):* The tree in India in Bodh Gaya under which the Buddha attained awakening.

Buddha (Skt.): The historical Buddha Gautama or Sakyamuni who lived 480–400 BCE, or any person who has realized the enlightenment found by Sakyamuni.

Chao-chou (778–897): Chinese Ch'an master; many *koan* stories originated from him.

Chi: Energy as understood in the Chinese tradition of medicine and martial arts.

Chogye Order: The Imjae Son order in Korea to which the nuns and monks, monasteries, and nunneries I mention belong.

Choson (1392–1910): The Neo-Confucianist Korean Yi Dynasty.

Dharma (Skt.): The teachings of Buddhism or a Buddha; the universal law, the way things are; a phenomenon.

Dharma exchange: In Zen Buddhism, a dialogue between a teacher and a student used to test the level of the student's understanding of the Dharma.

Dharmagupta: Ancient Indian Buddhist School from which the monastic rules of the Korean Chogye Order descend.

Dongguk University: Main Buddhist university in Seoul.

Doubt: In Zen Buddhism, the perplexed inquiry into the nature of one's existence.

Elder: For monks and nuns, the preceptor or preceptress of one's own preceptor or preceptress.

Gautama: One of the names of the Buddha, which comes from the name of his clan.

Haejae (K.): Free season; lit. "releasing the rule."

Hakuin Zenji (1689–1769): Japanese Rinzai Zen master.

Hanam, Zen Master(1876–1951): Korean Buddhist teacher renowned for his Zen practice, doctrinal learning, and adherence to the monastic precepts.

Huai Jang (677–744): Chinese Ch'an master.

Hui-neng (638–713): Sixth patriarch of the Chinese Ch'an tradition.

Hwadu (K.): Lit. "head of speech," i.e., the apex or point at which speech and thought are exhausted. The central point of a *koan* that is singled out as a topic of meditation, e.g., "What is this?" or "No!"

Hyanggok, Zen Master (n.d.): Teacher who supported the practice of Korean nuns.

Hyobong, Zen Master (1888–1966): Teacher of Master Kusan. He became a monk late in life after being a judge. Head of the Korean Buddhist Sangha 1962–66.

Imjae Son School: Main school of Korean Zen, using *koan* and *hwadu* practice.

Kalpa (Skt.): Aeons of varying length described in Buddhist cosmology.

Kangwon: Lecture hall.

Koan (Jap.): Lit. "public case"; the historical record of an exchange between a Zen master and a disciple or disciples.

Kobong, Zen Master (1890–1961): Dharma brother and successor of Master Mangong.

Kusan, Zen Master (1909–1983): Zen master of Songgwangsa who supported foreign monks and nuns to train in Korea.

Kyonbong, Zen Master (1892–1982): One of the most respected Korean Zen masters of this century. Renowned for his calligraphy.

Kyolche (K.): Meditation season; lit. "binding rule."

Lokeshvara (Skt.): See *Avalokiteshvara.*

Li (Ch.): A Chinese mile, approximately half a kilometer.

Linchi Ch'an School: Chinese Buddhist meditation school inspired by the great Ch'an master Linchi (d. 867).

Mahayana: Lit. "great vehicle." A name for the teachings of the Buddha that deal with the bodhisattva path to enlightenment. It is the form of Buddhism prevalent in China, Korea, Japan, and Tibet.

Mal (K.): A measure of weight used in Korea, approximately eighteen liters.

Man'gong, Zen Master (1872–1946): A great Korean Zen teacher active at the beginning of the century who did much to revitalize the Zen tradition and support nuns in their practice. He was also known for his liberal interpretation of the monastic rule.

Mansong, Zen Master (1897–1975): Nun who received transmission from Master Man'gong; renowned for her strict discipline and hard practice.

Manjushri (Skt.): A bodhisattva who personifies wisdom.

Moku (K.): Korean vegetable of which you only can eat the whitish stalk.

Mount Sumeru: The mountain that stands in the middle of the universe, according to Indian and Buddhist cosmology.

Nirvana (Skt.): The state of peace realized through the cessation of *samsara.*

Patriarch: In Zen Buddhism, someone who has served to transmit the direct insight of "mind to mind" from Sakyamuni via Bodhidharma down to the present day.

Paekche (18 BCE–668 CE): One of the three kingdoms of ancient Korea.

Perfections: Qualities that must be perfected in Mahayana Buddhism: generosity, morality, patience, effort, meditation, and wisdom.

Pikkuni (K.): Fully ordained Buddhist nun; also *bhiksuni.*

Pophui, Zen Master (1887–1974): Nun who received transmission from Master Man'gong; renowned for her humility and matter-of-factness about her accomplishments.

Postulant: Someone training to become a monk or nun, usually given menial chores in the monastery or nunnery. Postulancy usually lasts about a year.

Preceptress: The nun who accepts a postulant into her care for ordination.

Puril Pojo (1158–1210): Sometimes spelled Bojo and also known as Chinul, the founder of Songgwangsa.

Rinzai Zen School: Japanese school of Zen using *koan* practice.

Sa (K.): Monastery or nunnery (e.g., Songgwangsa: Songgwang Monastery).

Samsara (Skt.): The cycle of repeated birth and death; worldly existence in general.

Samadhi (Skt.): Meditative state of concentration.

Sanggi (K.): Rising of the *chi* to the head.

Sangha (Skt.): One's spiritual community in general; communities of one's fellow monks and nuns in particular.

Sarira (Skt.): Small mineral-like droplets of varying sizes and colors that are sometimes found among the cremated remains of monks, nuns, and other religious practitioners, which are then frequently enshrined and worshipped as sacred relics.

Shaolin (Ch.): Lit. "little forest"; reference to the name of the temple of Bodhidharma, the first Chinese Zen patriarch.

Silla (57 BCE–660 CE): One of the three kingdoms of ancient Korea.

Sramanerika: A novice nun with ten precepts.

Sunim (K.): The Korean title of address for monks and nuns.

Sutra (Skt.): A discourse delivered by the Buddha.

Stupa: A Buddhist reliquary.

Tanjon (K.): a point three finger-widths below the navel.

Theravada: Main Buddhist school found in South-East Asian countries like Thailand, Burma, and Sri Lanka.

Vairocana: The name of a Buddha whose body is said symbolically to constitute the universe.

Vimalakirti: A wise layman at the time of the Buddha whose teachings are recorded in the *Vimalakirti-nirdesa Sutra.*

Vinaya (Skt.): Ethical discipline. The body of ethical rules and disciplines for Buddhist monks and nuns prescribed by the Buddha.

Zen (Jap.; *Son* [K.]; *Ch'an* [Ch.]): Lit. "meditation." The name for the tradition of Buddhism emphasizing meditative practice that originated with Bodhidharma, Hui-neng, and others in China.

➤ Selected Readings

Batchelor, Martine. 1999. *Principles of Zen.* London: Thorsons.

————. 2000. "Jamin Sunim: Prison Work for a Korean Nun"; "Myohi Sunim: a Korean Nun Teacher of Elderly Women"; "Pomyong Sunim: Flower Arranging for the Korean Lay." In *Women's Buddhism, Buddhism's Women: Tradition, Revision, Renewal,* edited by Ellison Banks Findly, 275–81. Boston: Wisdom Publications.

————. 2000. "Tokwang Sunim: a Korean Nun as a Medical Practitioner." In *Women's Buddhism, Buddhism's Women: Tradition, Revision, Renewal,* edited by Ellison Banks Findly, 403–4. Boston: Wisdom Publications.

————. 2002. *Women on the Buddhist Path.* London: Thorsons.

————. 2004. *The Path of Compassion: The Bodhisattva Precepts.* Walnut Creek: Altamira.

Bongak Sunim. 2004. "Overcoming Tradition: Reconstructing and Transforming the Role of Korean Buddhist Nuns Through Education." In *Buddhist Woman and Social Justice,* edited by Karma Lekshe Tsomo, 265–67. Taipei: Yuan Chuan Press.

Buswell, Robert E., Jr., trans. 1991. *Tracing Back the Radiance.* Honolulu: Univ. of Hawaii Press.

————. 1992. *The Zen Monastic Experience: Buddhist Practice in Contemporary Korea.* Princeton: Princeton Univ. Press.

————, trans. 1993. "Arouse Your Mind and Practice." In *Sourcebook of Korean Civilization,* vol. 1, *From Early Times to the Sixteenth Century,* edited by Peter H. Lee et al., 154–57. New York: Columbia Univ. Press.

Chinul Sunim. 1981. "Advice for Beginners on the Way." Translated by Martine Fages; edited by Stephen Batchelor. Unpublished translation. Songgwangsa monastery, Suncheon, Republic of Korea.

Cho, Eunsu. 2004. "From Anonymity to Self-Reinvention: Korean Buddhist Nuns in the Twentieth Century." In *Buddhist Woman and Social Justice*, edited by Karma Lekshe Tsomo, 125–30. Taipei: Yuan Chuan Press.

Cleary, Christopher. 1977. *Swampland Flowers: The Letters and Lectures of Zen Master Ta Hui*. New York: Grove Press.

Cleary, Thomas. 1984. *The Flower Ornament Scripture (The Avatamsaka Sutra)*. Boston: Shambhala.

Cleary, Thomas, and J. C. Cleary, trans. 1977. *The Blue Cliff Record*. Boston: Shambhala.

Ha, Ch'unsaeng. 1988. "Han'guk ui Pikkuni" (Korean nuns). *Popbo Shin Mun* (Popbo newspaper), 4, 128.

Hakeda, Yoshito S., trans. 1967. *The Awakening of Faith*. New York: Columbia Univ. Press.

Hsieh, Ding-hwa Evelyn. 2004. " 'The Eight Chief Rules' in East Asian Mahayana Tradition: The Case of the Chinese Nuns' Order." Paper presented at the international conference Korean Nuns Within the Context of East Asian Buddhist Traditions, Hanmaum Seonwon, Anyang Shi, Republic of Korea.

Kabilsingh, Chatsumarn. 1984. *A Comparative Study of Bhikkuni Patimokkha*. Varanesi: Chaukhambha Orientalia.

Kusan Sunim. 1982. *Nine Mountains: Dharma-lectures of the Korean Meditation Master Ku San*. 4th ed. Chogye, Republic of Korea: International Meditation Center.

———. 1985. *The Way of Korean Zen*. Translated by Martine Fages; edited by Stephen Batchelor. New York: Weatherhill.

Lu K'uan Yu. 1960. *Ch'an and Zen Teachings*. London: Century Hutchinson.

Neungin Sunim. 2004. "Elder Care Programme Unifying Generations: The Case of Ilsan Elder Welfare Center in Korea." In *Buddhist Women and Social Justice*, edited by Karma Lekshe Tsomo, 243–46. Taipei: Yuan Chuan Press.

Pori Park. 2004. "Establishment of Buddhist Nunneries in Contemporary Korea." Paper presented at the international conference Korean Nuns Within the Context of East Asian Buddhist Traditions, Hanmaum Seonwon, Anyang Shi, Republic of Korea.

P'yonchipbu. 1983. "Mansongsonsa ui Haejang" (Records of the doings of female Zen Master Mansong), *Unmunhoebo* (Unmun bulletin), 1, 7.

Samu Sunim. 1986. "Manseong Sunim, a Women Zen Master of Modern Korea."

Spring Wind: Buddhist Cultural Forum 6, no. 1–3 (special issue on Women and Buddhism): 129–62.

Sogun Sunim. 2003. "The Bikkuni Sangha of the Three Kingdoms." Unpublished paper, private collection.

Son'gyong Sunim. 1986. "Mit Obnun Pae e Han P'yongsang ul Sitko" (Collection of poems of Son'gyong Sunim). Privately published. Myongpopsa nunnery, Republic of Korea.

Tsomo, Karma Lekshe, ed. 2004. "Discipline and Practice of Buddhist Women: Present and Past." Proceedings of the Eighth Sakyadhita International Conference on Buddhist Women, Seoul, Republic of Korea, June 27-July 2.

Wonhyo Sunim. 1981. "On Cultivating Determination to Practise." Translated by Martine Fages; edited by Stephen Batchelor. Unpublished translation. Songgwangsa monastery, Suncheon, Republic of Korea.

Yampolski, Philip B., trans. 1967. *The Platform Sutra of the Sixth Patriarch*. New York: Columbia Univ. Press.

Yaun Sunim. 1981. "On Self-Admonition." Translated by Martine Fages; edited by Stephen Batchelor. Unpublished translation. Songgwangsa monastery, Suncheon, Republic of Korea.